Written by Toby Glover©2023
@tobybooktour

Illustrated by Jes Vazquez
@ j.vazquez.prada

The author gives the purchaser permission to photocopy the phonic activities and flashcards for educational use.

Contents

Welcome to Groovy Phonics 3 1

How to use this book 2

What you'll need 3

Let's meet our new Groovy Friends 4

Let's Dance! 7

The Phonic Flower 9

Blending 10

Segmenting 11

Secret Words 12

Phonic Challenges 13

Structure 14

Set 10

/tr/   Tracy Train 16

/br/   Bradley Brown Bear 22

/cr/   Craig Crab 28

/fr/   Francis Treefrog 34

/gr/   Grandma Grace 40

/pr/   Princess Caprice 46

/dr/   Dragon Drake 52

I can read Set #10 58

Set 11

/cl/	Clara Clownfish	60
/fl/	Florence Flamingo	66
/gl/	Gloria Glitterbug	72
/pl/	Plastic Plane	78
/bl/	Blake Blowfish	84
/sl/	Sleepy Sloth	90
I can read Set #11		96

Set 12

/st/	Steve Stegosaurus	98
/sp/	Spencer Spider	104
/sk/	Skeleton Skip	110
/sc/	Scarlett Scout	116
/sm/	Smith Smew	122
/sn/	Sniffy Snowman	128
I can read Set #12		134

Groovy Phonics: Assessment 3 135
Groovy Friends flashcards 136
Secret Words 142

PHONICS

Welcome to Groovy Phonics 3

The key aim of Groovy Phonics is to teach children to read in a fun interactive way by promoting a seamless transition from decoding to reading. So far we have taught the initial sounds, some common digraphs and trigraphs, blending them together to make simple CVC words. We learnt non-phonetic secret words and read simple sentences fluently. In this book we shall meet new Groovy Friends as we learn about consonant digraphs, plus more secret words, and apply this new knowledge to read and write more complex sentences.

Just as in previous phases, the sounds will be represented by new Groovy Friends, cute alliterative characters each with their own fun rhyming song and accompanying funky dance moves. Alliteration and rhyme are very important as they develop children's ability to tune into speech sounds. This is especially important for those learning English as an additional language both domestically and in international schools abroad.

Music plays a fundamental role in developing children's language. Groovy Phonics allows children to develop a broad repertoire of songs, each with multi-sensory actions and dance moves which encourage them to move in certain ways. This type of mnemonic learning is an excellent way to learn in a quick, memorable and, most important of all, fun way.

How to use this book

Each new digraph is accompanied by a clear and precise lesson plan, showing how to teach it following this simple pattern:

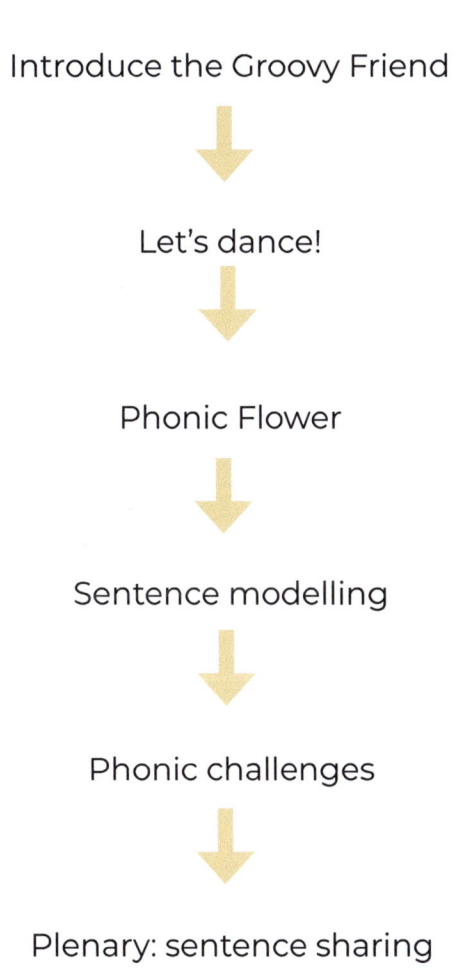

Introduce the Groovy Friend

⬇

Let's dance!

⬇

Phonic Flower

⬇

Sentence modelling

⬇

Phonic challenges

⬇

Plenary: sentence sharing

What you'll need

Songs: All available free at www.groovyphonics.com just scan the QR code below.

Groovy Friend flashcards: These are at the back of this book, to cut out and laminate so children can blend them together like puzzles to read words.

Phonic Challenges: Make photocopies to save cutting the book to pieces.

Stationery: Pencils, colours, plus it would be great to have a mini whiteboard and some dry-wipe marker pens so that children can practise forming the letters independently.

Patience: 15-20 minutes a day is plenty! But don't insist on it; some children will happily work longer, some may become restless.

Ear-plugs: I guarantee that after a few weeks the songs will drive you crazy... especially when you catch yourself singing them in the shower!

Meet the Groovy Friends

In this book we will teach the Phase 4 consonant blends which are predominantly found at the beginning of words. These are composed of three main blends: r-controlled; l-controlled; and s-controlled.

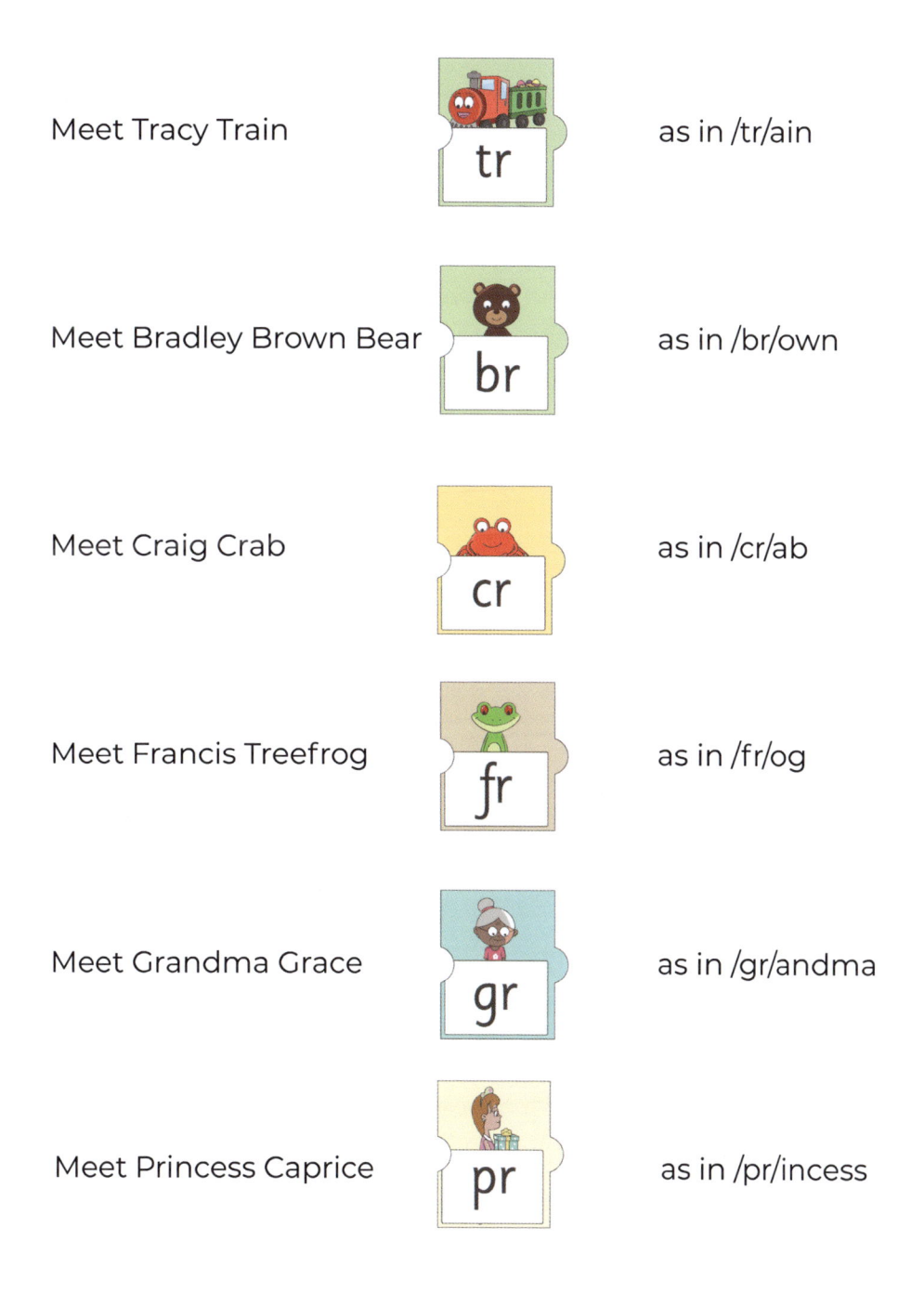

Meet Tracy Train — **tr** — as in /tr/ain

Meet Bradley Brown Bear — **br** — as in /br/own

Meet Craig Crab — **cr** — as in /cr/ab

Meet Francis Treefrog — **fr** — as in /fr/og

Meet Grandma Grace — **gr** — as in /gr/andma

Meet Princess Caprice — **pr** — as in /pr/incess

Meet Dragon Drake — **dr** — as in /dr/agon

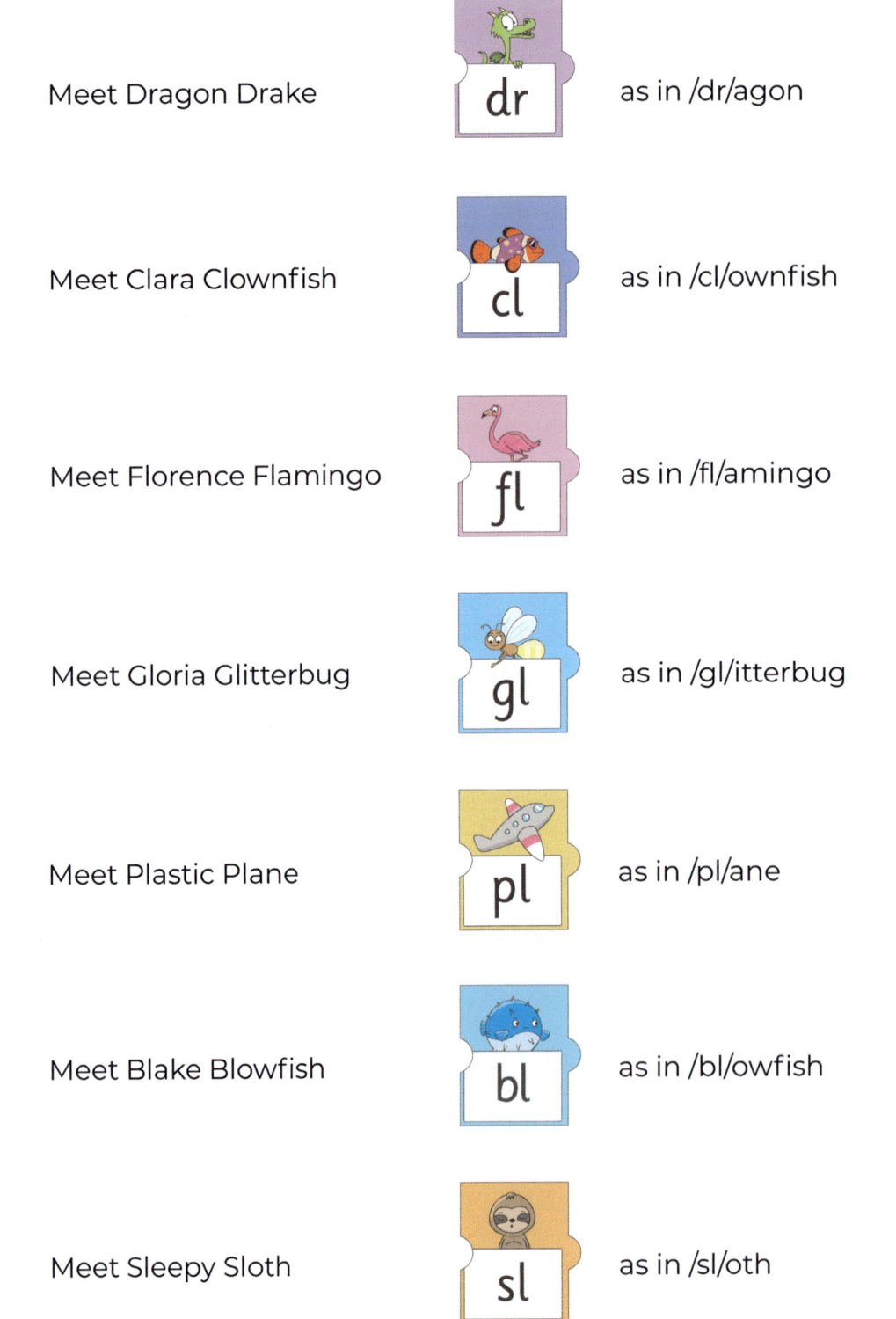

Meet Clara Clownfish — **cl** — as in /cl/ownfish

Meet Florence Flamingo — **fl** — as in /fl/amingo

Meet Gloria Glitterbug — **gl** — as in /gl/itterbug

Meet Plastic Plane — **pl** — as in /pl/ane

Meet Blake Blowfish — **bl** — as in /bl/owfish

Meet Sleepy Sloth — **sl** — as in /sl/oth

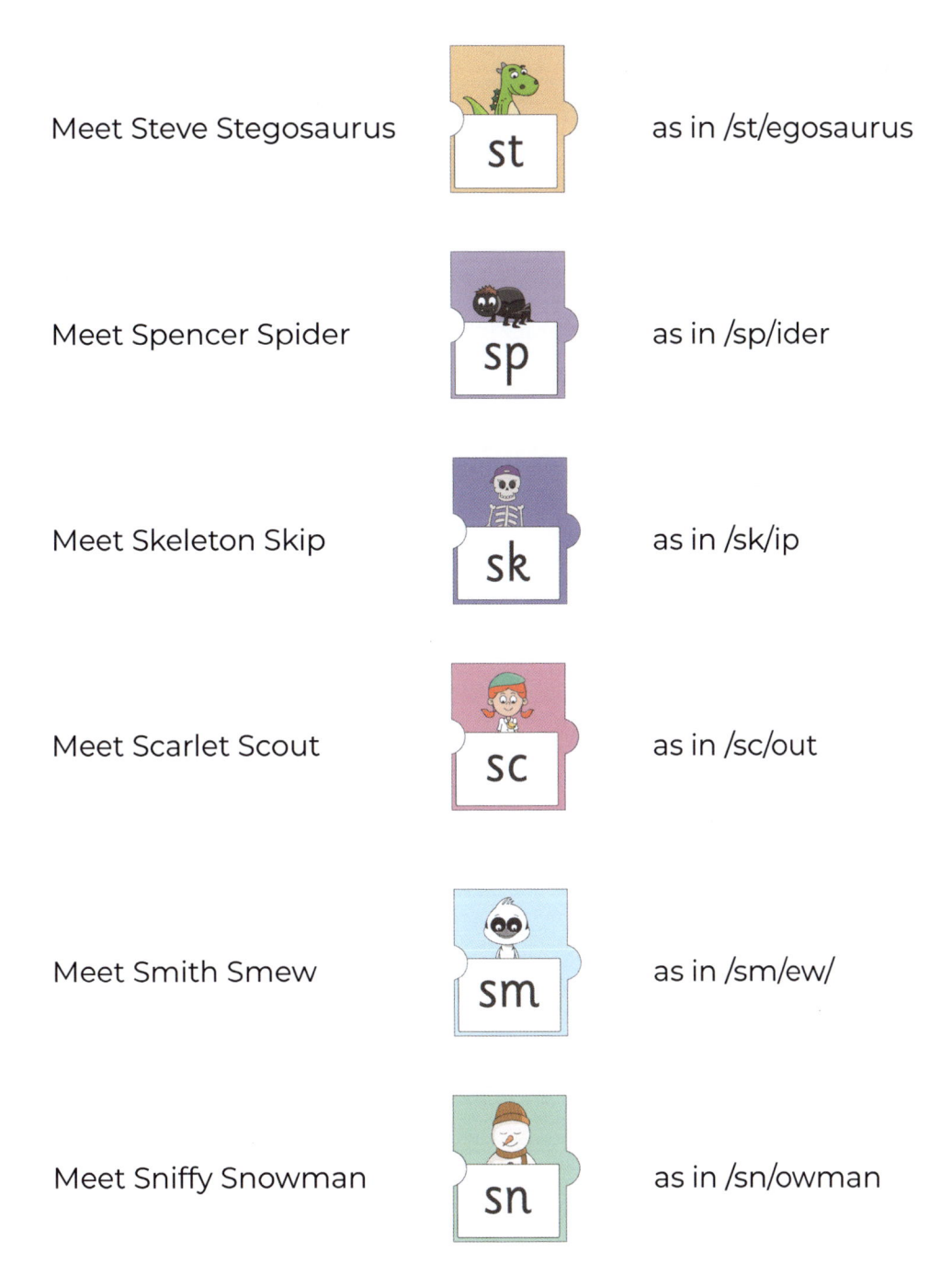

Meet Steve Stegosaurus	**st**	as in /st/egosaurus
Meet Spencer Spider	**sp**	as in /sp/ider
Meet Skeleton Skip	**sk**	as in /sk/ip
Meet Scarlet Scout	**sc**	as in /sc/out
Meet Smith Smew	**sm**	as in /sm/ew/
Meet Sniffy Snowman	**sn**	as in /sn/owman

This type of mnemonic learning is a fun, child-friendly way to enhance memory and reinforce the sounds. Once children become more familiar with the sounds, they will no longer need to rely on the Groovy Friends and will learn to identify them by sight. Hence, the flashcards at the back of this book are reversable, with the Groovy Friend and sound on one side, and just the sound on the other.

Let's Dance!

As mentioned, music plays a vital part in developing children's language. Each Groovy Friend has its own catchy, rhyming and alliterative song, accompanied by fun, multi-sensory dance move. Remember to reinforce that we only perform a dance move when we hear the digraph in question. Play the songs together a few times, then use the model on the next page to teach the words and actions.

It is important to slow the tempo of the song as you model how to sing. This will help children understand the lyrics, while the slower pace will afford more time to sync the words with the actions. As they gain confidence, you can increase the tempo to match the videos as you sing along. It is also fun to add musical instruments, such as shakers and tambourines.

Groovy Tip: It is fun to experiment with the tone of your voice; try singing one line quiet, the next line loud; varying the pace and pitch: fast and slow, high and low.

Read aloud the first line

⬇

Encourage children to repeat it

⬇

Repeat the line modelling the dance moves

⬇

Have the children copy

⬇

Now sing the first line with the actions

⬇

Have the children repeat

⬇

Now repeat the same sequence with the next four lines

⬇

Sing the whole song together with the video

Phonic Flower

Once familiar with the song and dance moves, it's time for the Phonic Flower. Let's use Steve Stegosaurus as an example. Draw a circular flower bud with **/st/** in the middle, then surround it with petals. Encourage the children to think of some words featuring the /st/ sound. Mime the dance moves from the song, then encourage children to recall the associated word, placing emphasis on the digraph i.e. /st/-o-p. Each time they think of a word, add it to the petals, like so:

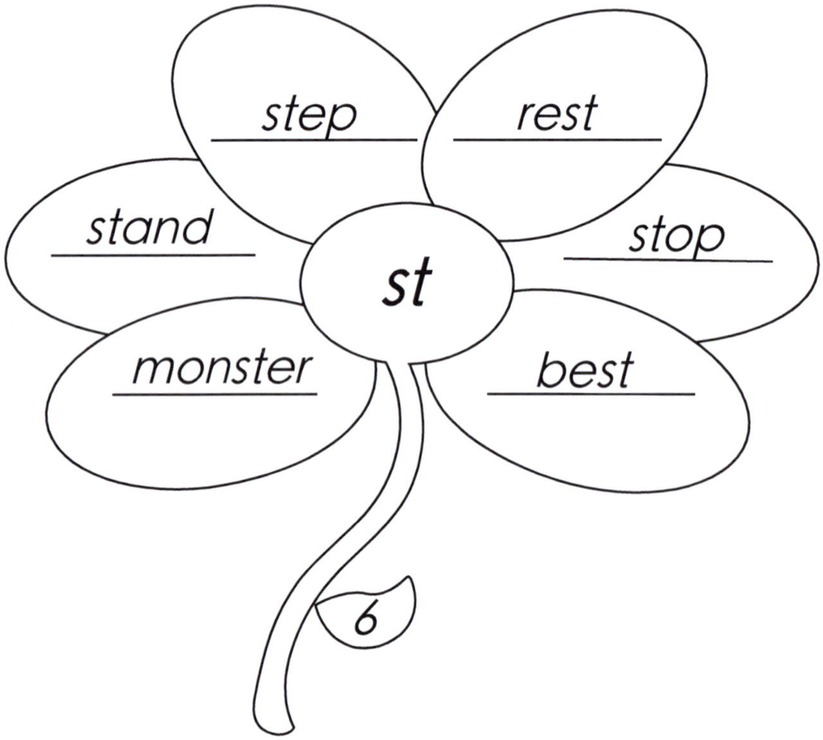

step
rest
stand
st
stop
monster
best
6

Each lesson plan includes five prompter questions to encourage children to think of words featuring the digraphs in context. The goal is to fill all the petals, then add even more.

Blending

As these new digraphs are learnt, children can join them together with previously taught sounds to decode longer words. This is called blending.

Phase 4 sounds will usually be found at the beginning of words and fall into three categories:

Digraphs blending with /r/:

tr i p   cr a b

Digraphs blending with /l/:

sl ee p   fl a t

Digraphs blending with /s/:

sk i p   st o p

Segmenting

Segmenting is the reverse of blending and the perfect way to teach young children how to spell. Once children are able to blend and read common words, they will be able to recognise the sounds that form them. Children then apply this knowledge when attempting to spell decodable words indepedently by sounding them out as they write. The Phonic Challenges provide a perfect way to assess how they are progressing with spelling.

It is a great idea to have a mini whiteboard and some dry-wipe pens to allow children the opportuntity to attempt to write words independently. Children loves to write in pen as it makes them feel very grown up; let them choose any colour too.
Let's make writing fun!

Groovy Tip: Once blending and segmenting have been introduced to children, they should be taught together as the processes are reversible.

Secret Words

As discussed in the previous books, the English language is not composed exclusively of decodable sounds all neatly blended together to form words. Once again these non-decodable *secret words* are available at the end of the book to be cut out and laminated.

Phase 2 secret words
is I the put pull full as and his her has no go to into she push he of we me be
Phase 3 secret words
was you they my by all are sure pure
Phase 4 secret words
said so have like some come love do were here little says there when what one out today

Whenever possible these words will be subtely introduced in the *I Can Read* assessment sheets. By introducing these *secret words* alongside familiar decodable words, children will learn them almost subliminally.

Groovy Tip: It is fun to print two copies of the secret words, then play a memory/snap game, have them face down on the table, then take turns flipping them over to collect pairs.

Phonic Challenges

These may be photocopied for multiple use.

Superstars

These five pointed stars each feature an image with the taught digraph. Beneath are phonic prompters, a dot for a single letter and a digraph dash on which they write the word.

Some examples: __ __ (tr ee)   __ . . (tr a p)   __ __ . (tr ai n)

Phonic flower

The phonic flower challenges children further by writing words *without* the prompters.

Sentence modelling

Both activities challenge the children to write a sentence of their own using the taught digraph. Each lesson plan has a sentence to model on the board emphasising:

1. Capital letter for the beginning of a sentence.
2. Finger space between each word.
3. A full-stop (period) at the end of the sentence.

Leave the sentence on the board as they work independently. Some children may copy the exact same sentence from the board. However, this is fine, the objective is to become accustomed with sentence structure. As they gain confidence they will compose sentences of their own. During the plenary invite children to read aloud their sentences and challenge peers to identify the digraphs in context.

Structure

The digraphs will be covered in three sets corresponding to the letter they blend with, namely /r/, /l/ and /s/. Each set concludes with a carefully structured reading activities which allow children to see the sounds in context in phonetic sentences integrated with *secret words*.

They will continue from the nine sets covered in the previous books:

Set 10	tr	br	cr	fr	gr	pr	dr
Set 11	cl	fl	gl	pl	bl	sl	
Set 12	st	sp	sk	sc	sm	sn	

s e t

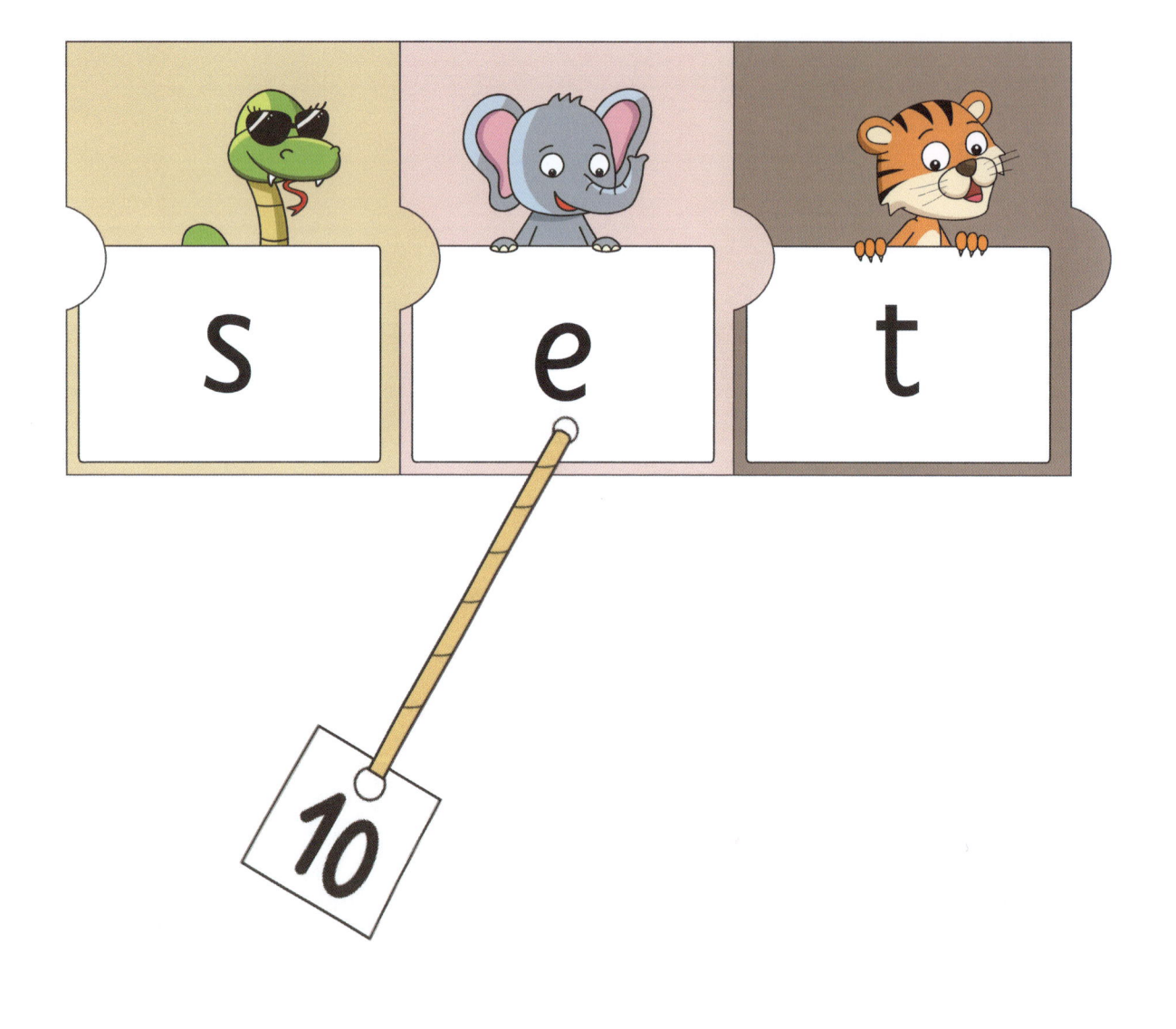

10

Lesson plan /tr/ Tracy Train

Show our Groovy Friends Tommy Tiger and Rachel Rabbit, explain how they blend together to make our new Groovy Friend /tr/ Tracy Train.

We find the **/tr/** sound: **mostly** at the start /tr/ee/
rarely inside con/tr/act
never at the end

Song and dance

Teach the song and dance a line at a time as detailed on page 8.

Phonic flower prompters

On Hallowe'en we say trick or...	*treat*
If it is not false, it is...	*true*
To catch a mouse we set a...	*trap*
A farmer drives a...	*tractor*
A dinosaur with three horns is a...	*Triceratops*

Sentence modelling

Model this sentence, focus on capital letter, finger spaces and full-stop.

The train travels on tracks.

Hand out the Phonic Challenges as Tracy Train plays on repeat.

Plenary

Invite children to read out their sentences. Can anyone identify the /tr/ word?

| tr | br cr fr gr pr dr | cl fl gl pl bl sl | st sp sk sc sm sn |

tr

tr ee

tr i ck

tr i p

tr ai n

Tracy Train

Tracy train travels triangle tracks

Tugging treasure filled trucks and trendy hats

No traffic trouble

Just trees by the double

While Troy plays the trumpet (that's her cat!)

| tr | br cr fr gr pr dr | cl fl gl pl bl sl | st sp sk sc sm sn |

1. train	2. triangle	3. treasure	4. truck
5. trouble	6. trees	7. trumpet	

1	Make a **train** action with your straight hands by your side.
2	Make a **triangle** with your fingers and thumbs.
3	Rub your hands together for **treasure**.
4	Pretend to be driving a big **truck**.
5	Head in your hands for **trouble**.
6	Hands above your head for **tree**.
7	Pretend to be playing a **trumpet**.

Groovy Phonics

This /tr/ superstar is called.....................................

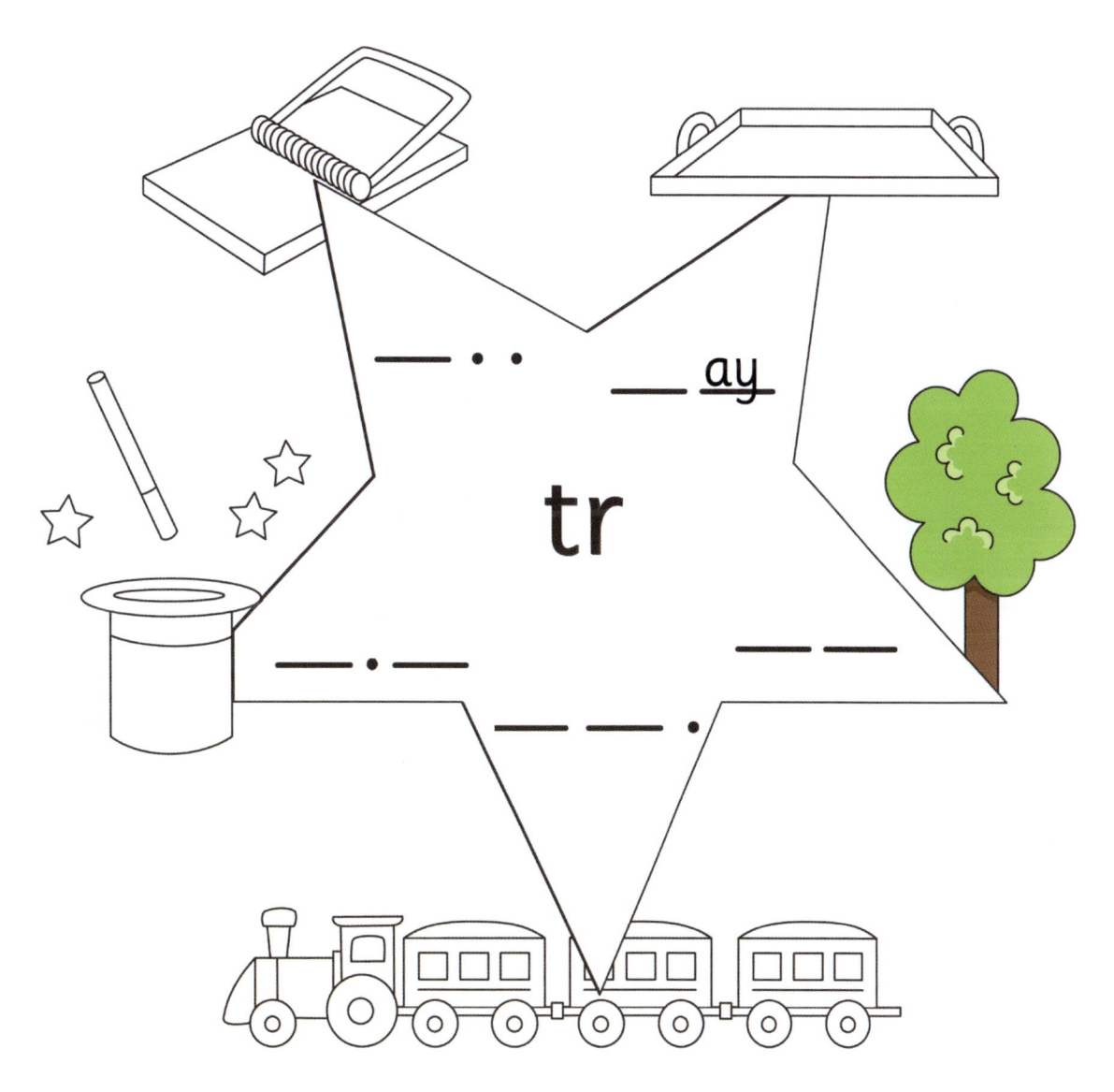

tr

Let's write a sentence using /tr/

_____

_____

Phonic flower

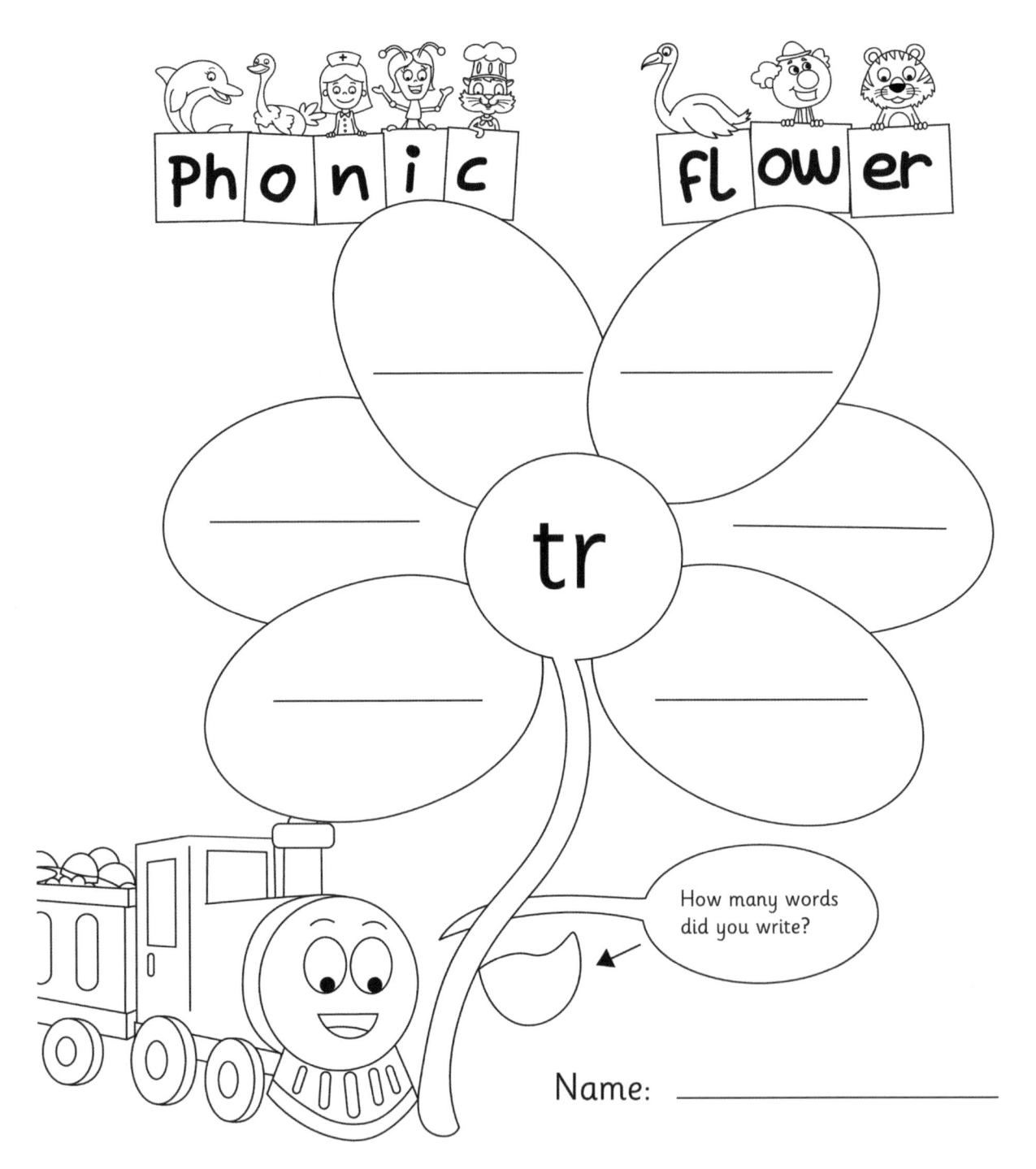

tr

How many words did you write?

Name: _____

Let's write a sentence using /tr/

_____
_____

21

Lesson plan /br/ Bradley Brown Bear

Show our Groovy Friends Barry Bat and Rachel Rabbit, explain how they blend together to make our new Groovy Friend /br/ Bradley Brown Bear.

We find the **/br/** sound: **mostly** at the start /br/u/sh
rarely inside em/br/ace
never at the end

Song and dance

Teach the song and dance a line at a time as detailed on page 8.

Phonic flower prompters

The third little pig made his house out of…	*bricks*
To stop your bike, you pull the…	*brakes*
A witch flies on a…	*broom*
If you drop an egg it will…	*break*
Inside our head is our….	*brain*

Sentence modelling

Model this sentence, focus on capital letter, finger spaces and full-stop.

I have brown bread for breakfast.

Hand out the Phonic Challenges as Bradley Brown Bear plays on repeat.

Plenary

Invite children to read out their sentences. Can anyone recognise the /br/ word?

| tr | br | cr | fr | gr | pr | dr | | cl | fl | gl | pl | bl | sl | | st | sp | sk | sc | sm | sn |

br

br igh t

br i ng

br u sh

br ai n

Bradley Brown Bear

Bradley Brown Bear loves broccoli pie

And bronze bread for breakfast made from rye

He lives under a bridge

By the bright broken fridge

And brushes his fur every night

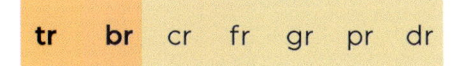

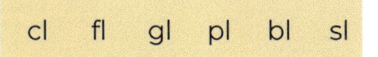

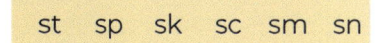

1.	brown bear
2.	breakfast
3.	bridge
4.	bright
5.	broken
6.	brush

1	Make hand claws like **Bradley Brown Bear**.
2	Rub your tummy, mmm... **bread** for **breakfast**.
3	Join your hands above your head to make a hand **bridge**.
4	Shield your eyes... so **bright**.
5	Hand on your brow, oh no, it's **broken**.
6	Paint with a **brush**.

Groovy Phonics

This /br/ superstar is called..................................

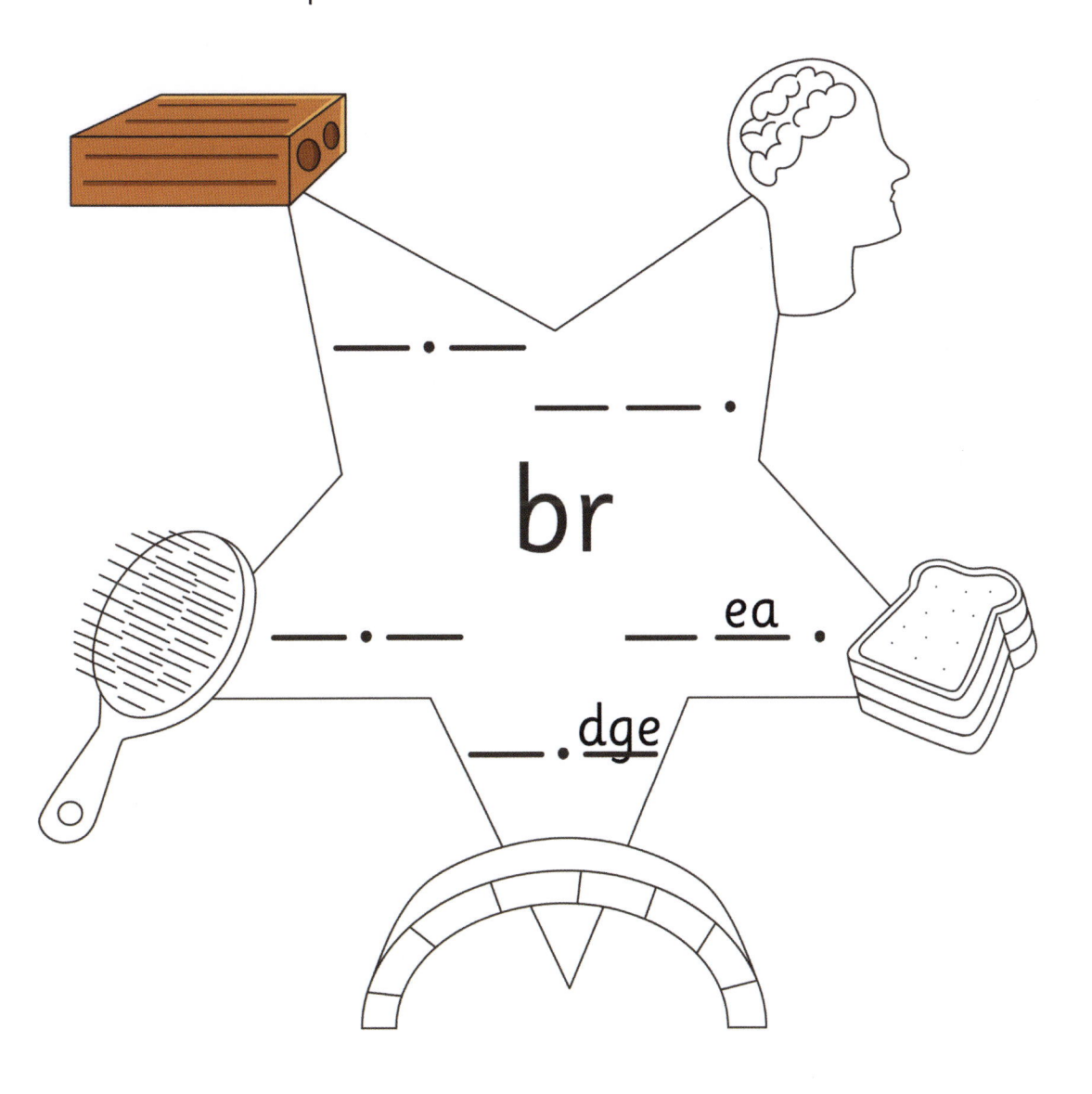

br

_ _ . _
_ _ _ .
_ . _
_ _ ea .
_ _ .dge

Let's write a sentence using /br/

_____

_____

Phonic Flower

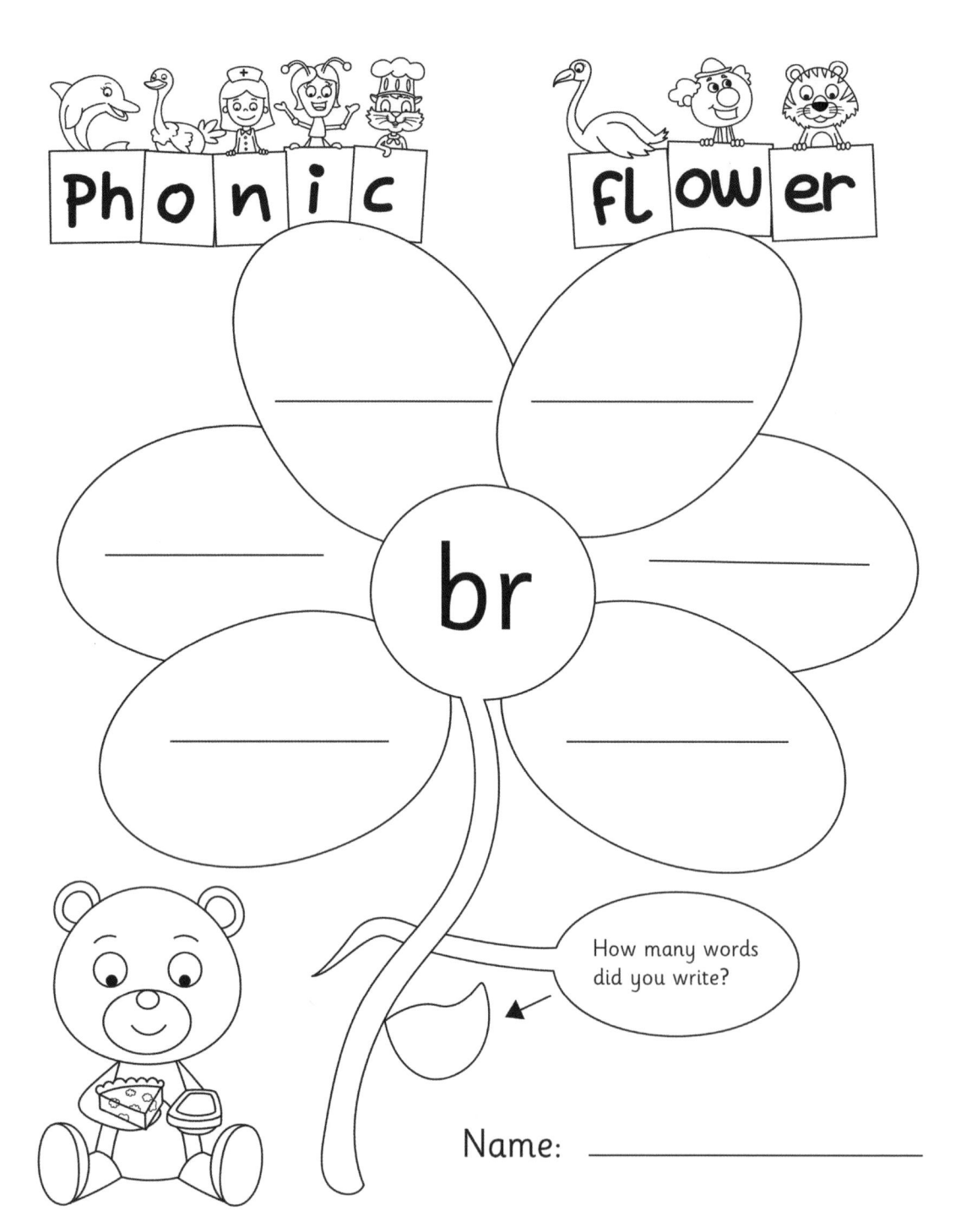

br

How many words did you write?

Name: _____

Let's write a sentence using /br/

27

Lesson plan /cr/ Craig Crab

Hold up our Groovy Friends Casey Cat and Rachel Rabbit, explain how they blend together to make our new Groovy Friend /cr/ Craig Crab.

We find the **/cr/** sound: **mostly** at the start /cr/ib
rarely inside con/cr/ete
never at the end

Song and dance

Teach the song and dance a line at a time as detailed on page 8.

Phonic flower prompters

We can draw a picture with a...	*crayon*
On his head, a king wears a...	*crown*
If you tap an egg it will...	*crack*
If you are upset you might...	*cry*
A sports game with a bat and a red ball is...	*cricket*

Sentence modelling

Model this sentence, focus on capital letter, finger spaces and full-stop.

The crab crawls across the sand.

Hand out the Phonic Challenges as Craig Crab plays on repeat.

Plenary

Invite children to read out their sentences. Can anyone identify the /cr/ word?

tr br cr fr gr pr dr   cl fl gl pl bl sl   st sp sk sc sm sn

cr

cr ow

cr o ss

cr a ck

cr u n ch

Craig Crab

Craig Crab plays criss-cross with a teacher

Mrs. Croc, an incredible creature

They crunch ice cream

A minty crisp dream

Craig cries like crazy, he can't beat her

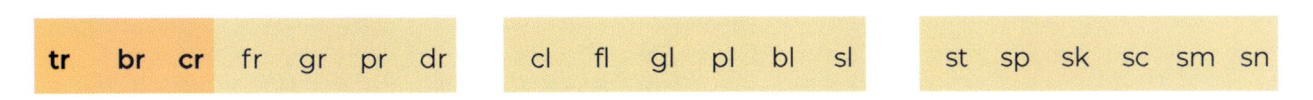

tr　br　cr　fr　gr　pr　dr　　　cl　fl　gl　pl　bl　sl　　　st　sp　sk　sc　sm　sn

1	Make snappy hand pincers like **Craig Crab**.
2	Make an /x/ with your hands to **criss-cross**.
3	Make snappy arm jaws like a **croc**.
4	Raise your hands in shock... so **incredible!**
5	Pretend to be eating some delicious **ice-cream**.
6	Pretend to **cry**.

Groovy Phonics

This /cr/ superstar is called..................................

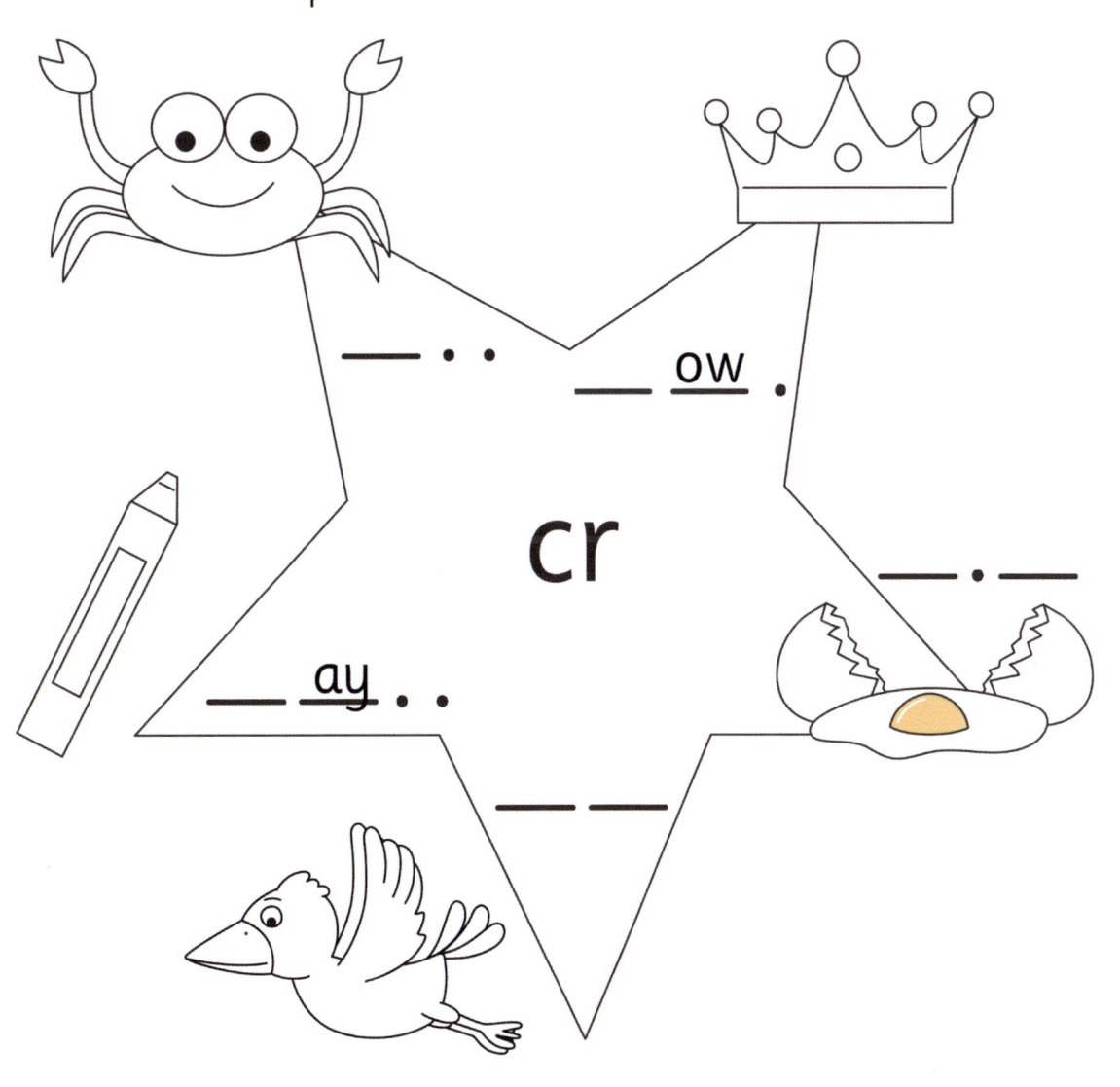

_ _ . .

_ ow .

cr

_ . _

_ ay . .

_ _

Let's write a sentence using /cr/

_____

_____

32

Phonic flower

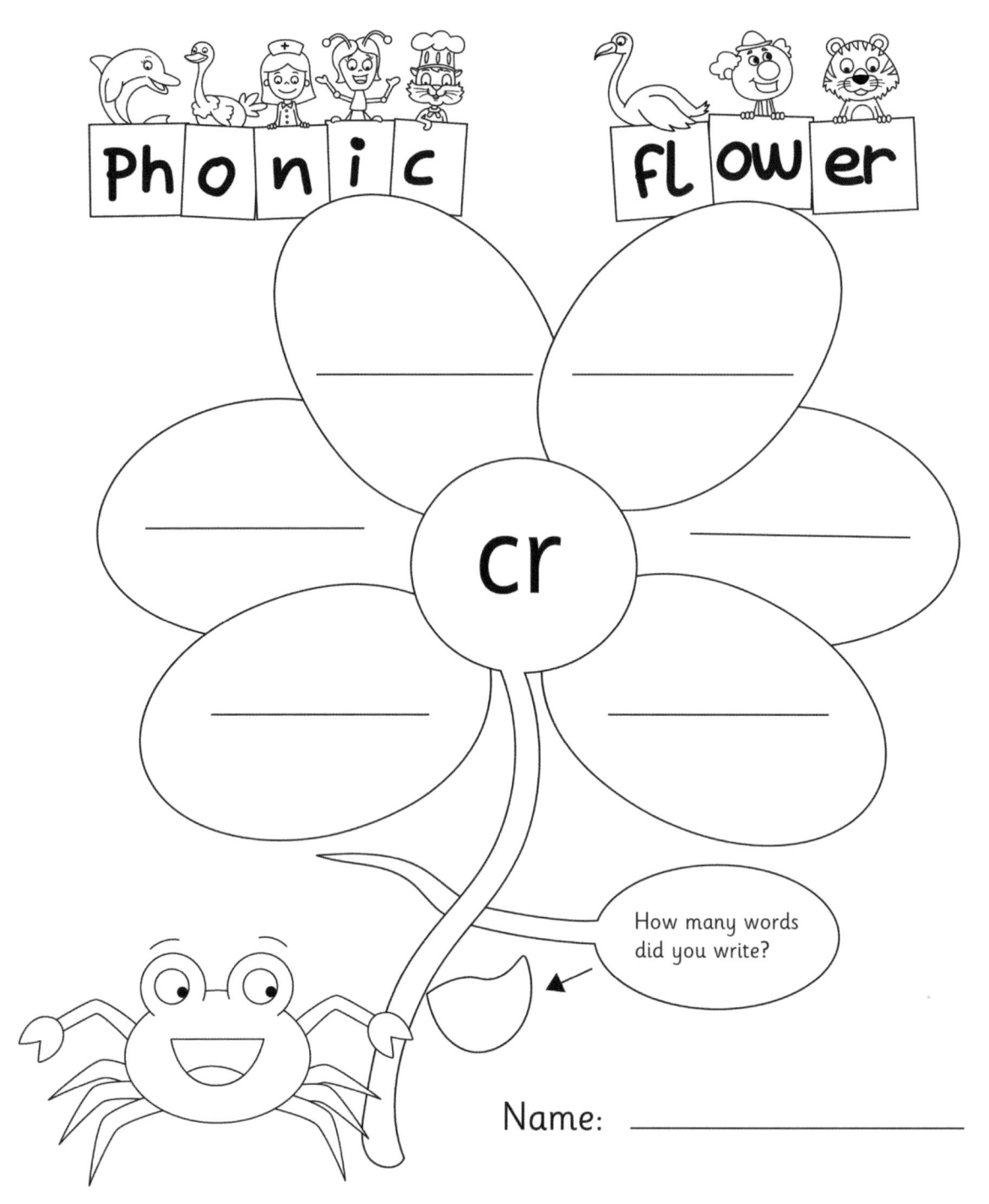

cr

How many words did you write?

Name: _____

Let's write a sentence using /cr/

_____

_____

Lesson plan /fr/ Francis Treefrog

Hold up our Groovy Friends Freddie Frog and Rachel Rabbit, explain how they blend together to make our new Groovy Friend /fr/ Francis Treefrog.

We find the **/fr/** sound: **mostly** at the start /fr/ee/
                                rarely inside a/fr/aid
                                never at the end

Song and dance

Teach the song and dance a line at a time as detailed on page 8.

Phonic flower prompters

In winter some ponds might...	*freeze*
The day after Thursday is...	*Friday*
The opposite of back is...	*front*
The Eiffel Tower is in...	*France*
Portraits in galleries have a...	*frame*

Sentence modelling

Model this sentence, focus on capital letter, finger spaces and full-stop.

The frog eats fruit.

Hand out the Phonic Challenges as Francis Treefrog plays on repeat.

Plenary

Invite children to read out their sentences. Can anyone identify the /fr/ word?

| tr | br | cr | **fr** | gr | pr | dr | | cl | fl | gl | pl | bl | sl | | st | sp | sk | sc | sm | sn |

fr

fr ee

fr o g

fr e sh

fr o m

Francis Treefrog

Francis Treefrog loves frosty fruit pie

Always front in line to order French fries

Fridge fresh and plenty

He frowns if it's empty

But his friends prefer sugar-free flies

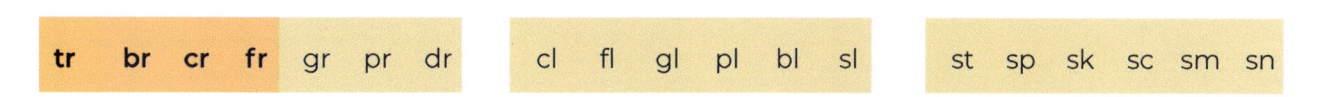

| tr br cr fr gr pr dr | cl fl gl pl bl sl | st sp sk sc sm sn |

1. treefrog	2. frosty	3. front	4. french fries

5. fridge	6. frowns	7. friends

1	Make googly eyes with your fists like **Francis Treefrog**.
2	Hug yourself warm, so **frosty**.
3	Put your palms out in **front**.
4	Pretend to be eating **French fries**.
5	Hug yourself warm again, for **fridge**.
6	Thumbs down for **frowns**.
7	Thumbs up for **friends**.

Groovy Phonics

This /fr/ superstar is called..................................

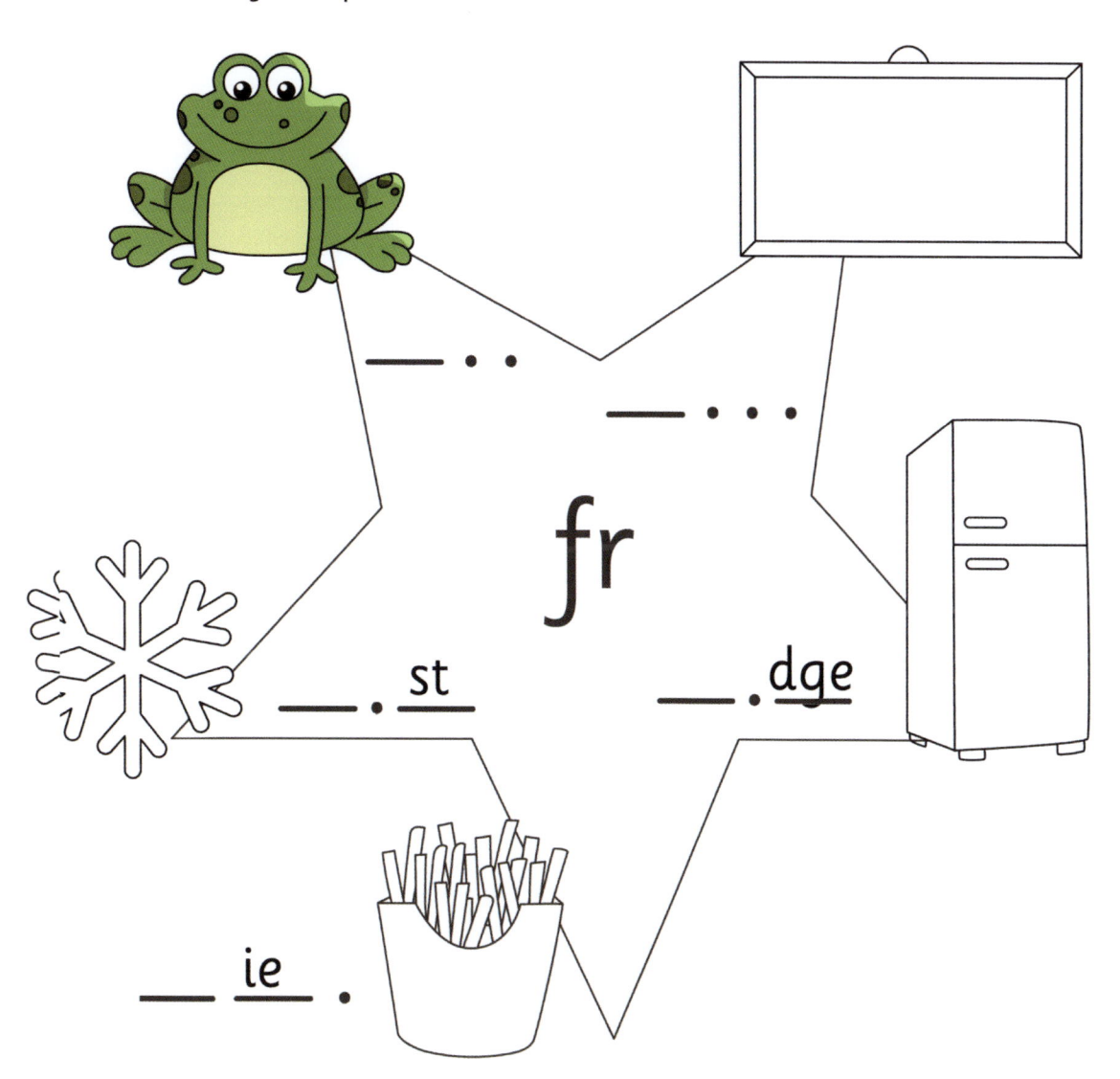

fr

__ __ . . (frog)

__ __ . . . (frame)

__ . st (frost)

__ . dge (fridge)

__ ie . (fries)

Let's write a sentence using /fr/

_____

_____

Phonic flower

fr

How many words did you write?

Name: _____

Let's write a sentence using /fr/

_____
_____

39

Lesson plan /gr/ Grandma Grace

Hold up our Groovy Friends Gaby Goat and Rachel Rabbit, explain how they blend together they make our new Groovy Friend /gr/ Grandma Grace.

We find the **/gr/** sound: **mostly** at the start /gr/in
                                   rarely inside a/gr/ee
                                   never at the end

Song and dance

Teach the song and dance a line at a time as detailed on page 8.

Phonic flower prompters

A cheeky smile is called a…	*grin*
A scary wolf might…	*growl*
A great big bear is a…	*grizzly*
The creature who stole Christmas is the…	*Grinch*
Rain falls on the…	*ground*

Sentence modelling

Model this sentence, focus on capital letter, finger spaces and full-stop.

Grandma grows green grapes.

Hand out the Phonic Challenges as Grandma Grace plays on repeat.

Plenary

Invite children to read out their sentences. Can anyone identify the /gr/ word?

tr br cr fr gr pr dr   cl fl gl pl bl sl   st sp sk sc sm sn

gr

gr ow

gr i p

gr ee n

gr i n

41

Grandma Grace

Grandma Grace has fingers so green

She loves to grow grapes, loves to grow beans

The grass on her land

So great and so grand

The grooviest grannie you ever have seen

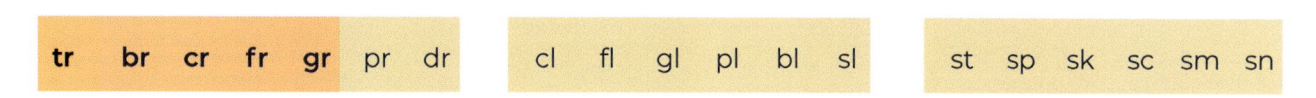

tr br cr fr gr pr dr   cl fl gl pl bl sl   st sp sk sc sm sn

1. green   2. grow   3. grapes
4. grow   5. grass   6. great   7. groovy

1	Point to something **green**.
2	Raise your palm in front of you, watch it **grow**.
3	Pretend to eat **green grapes**.
4	Raise your palm in front of you again, watch it **grow**.
5	Wiggle your fingers like **green grass**.
6	Thumbs up, so **great** and **grand**.
7	Do a reverse 'V' sign, so **groovy**!

Groovy Phonics

This /gr/ superstar is called..................................

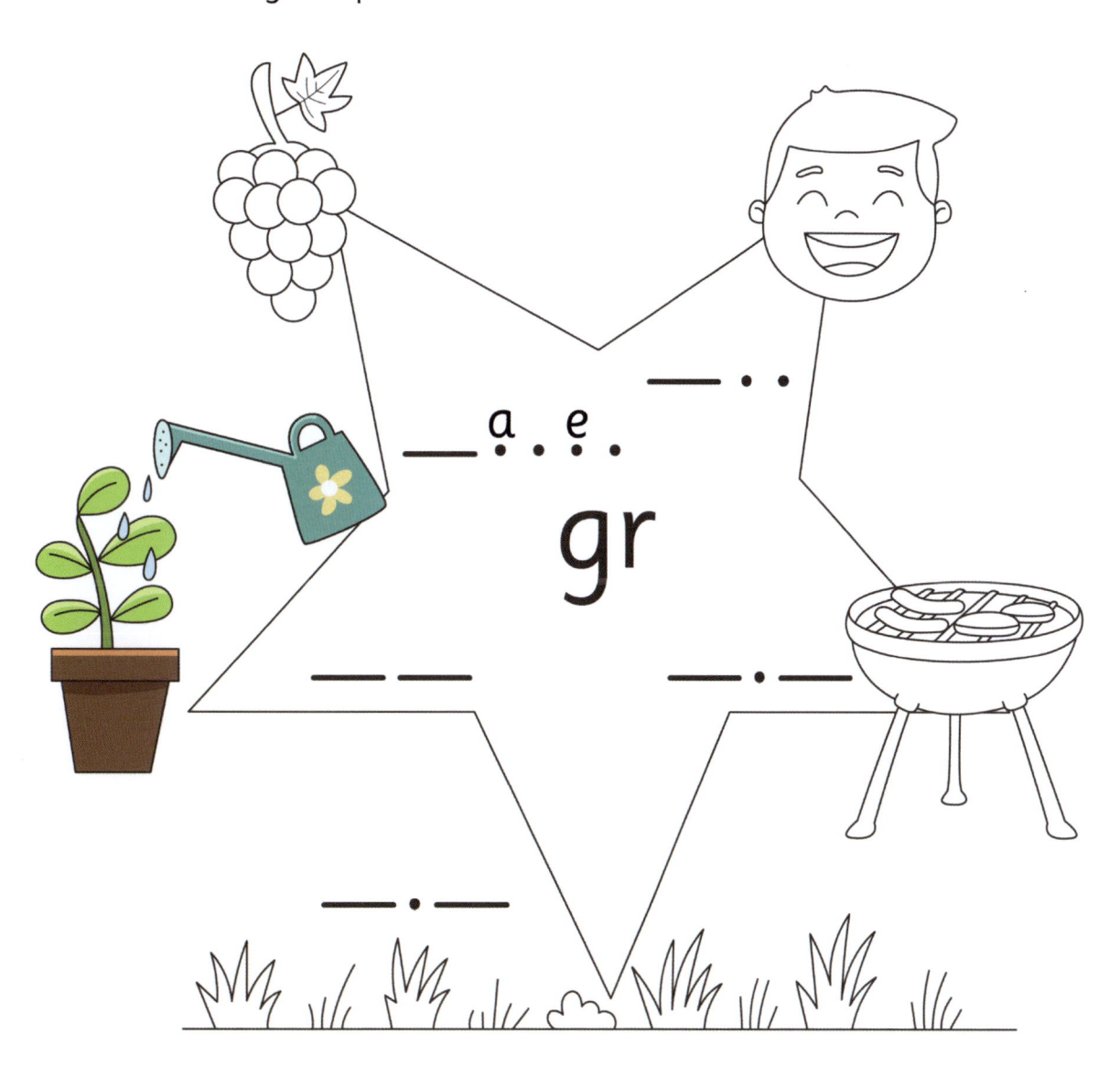

gr

Let's write a sentence using /gr/

_____

_____

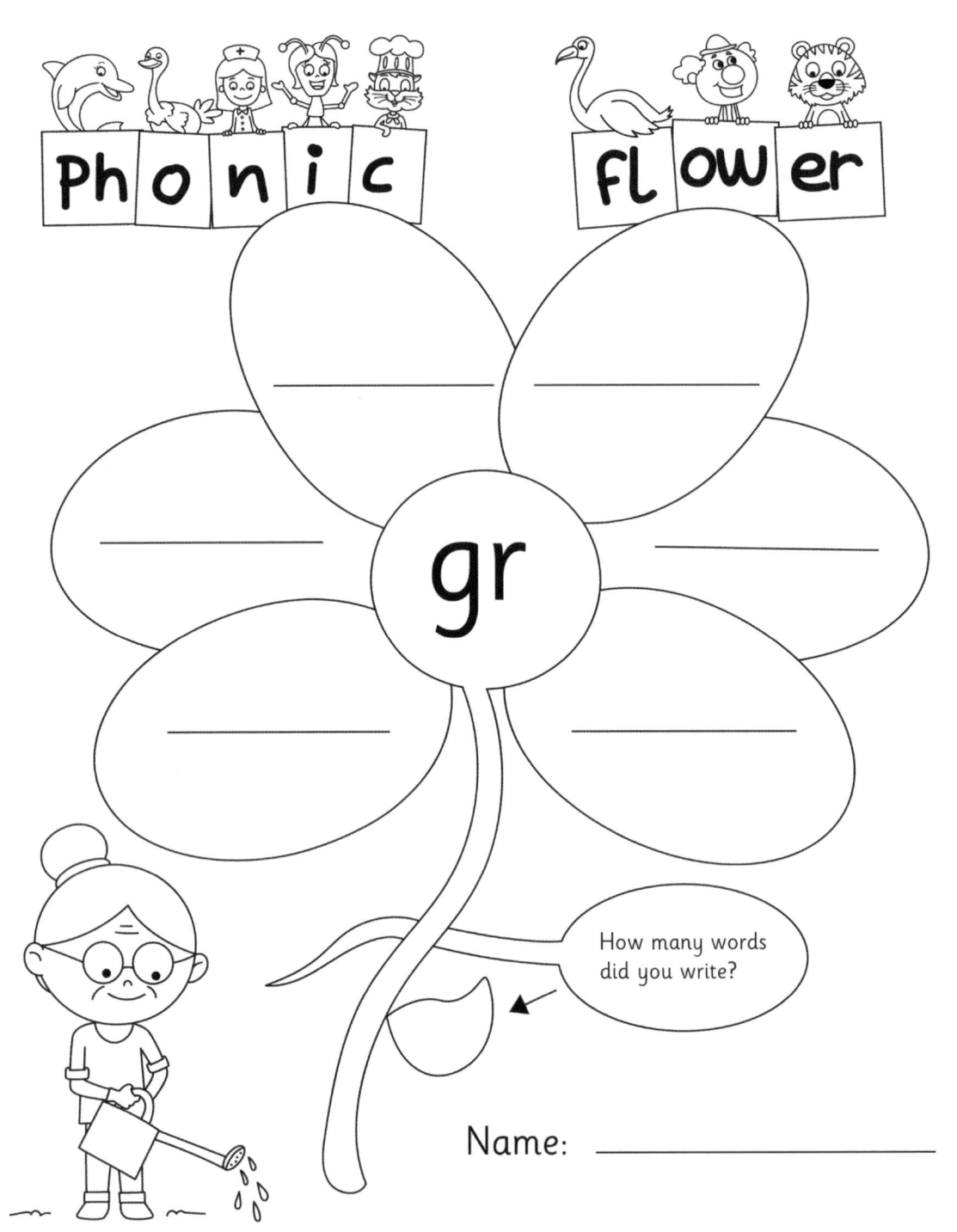

Phonic flower

gr

How many words did you write?

Name: _____

Let's write a sentence using /gr/

_____

_____

Lesson plan /pr/ Princess Caprice

Hold up our Groovy Friends Penny Piglet and Rachel Rabbit, explain how they blend together to make our new Groovy Friend /pr/ Princess Caprice.

We find the **/pr/** sound: **mostly** at the start /pr/am
  rarely inside im/pr/ess
  never at the end

Song and dance

Teach the song and dance a line at a time as detailed on page 9.

Phonic flower prompters

If you win a contest you might win a…	*prize*
We can push a baby in a…	*pram*
If something is difficult is it a…	*problem*
To ring the doorbell we have to…	*press*
We can draw a picture on a computer, then click…	*print*

Sentence modelling

Model this sentence, focus on capital letter, finger spaces and full-stop.

The pretty princess won a prize.

Hand out the Phonic Challenges as Princess Caprice plays on repeat.

Plenary

Invite children to read out their sentences. Can anyone identify the /pr/ word?

tr br cr fr gr pr dr   cl fl gl pl bl sl   st sp sk sc sm sn

pr

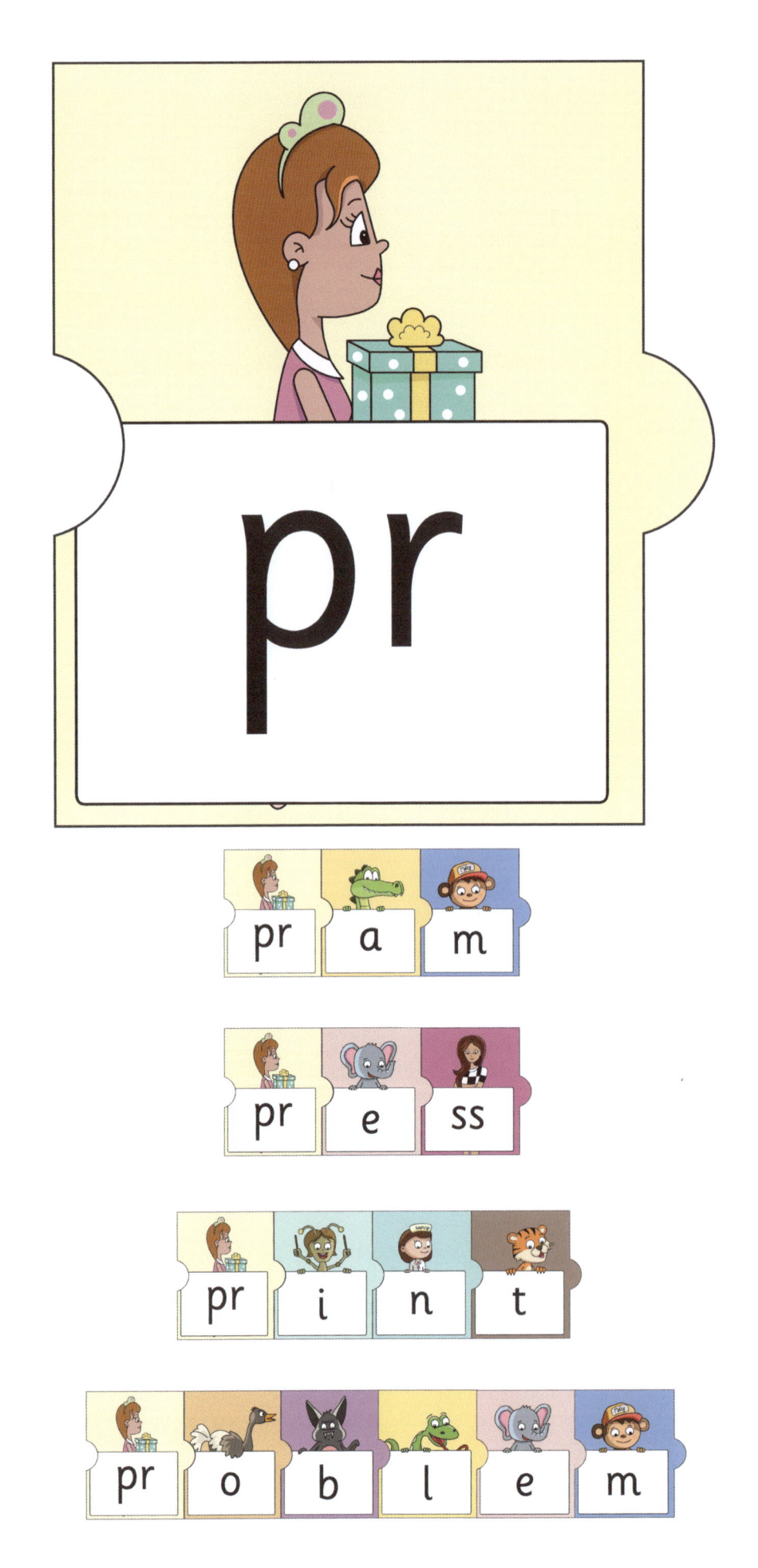

pr a m

pr e ss

pr i n t

pr o b l e m

47

Princess Caprice

Princess Caprice so pretty and nice

Longed to marry Prince Presley at any price

She gave him presents and gifts

Of king prawns and prime ribs

Which is probably why Presley doubled in size

| tr br cr fr gr pr dr | cl fl gl pl bl sl | st sp sk sc sm sn |

| 1. princess | 2. pretty | 3. prince |
| 4. present | 5. prawns | 6. probably |

1	Make a hand crown like a **princess**.
2	Hands on your cheeks, so **pretty**.
3	Make another hand crown like a **prince**.
4	Hands out in front like you are giving someone a **present**.
5	Rub tummy for **prawns** and **prime** ribs.
6	Wave your hand horizontally for **probably**.

Groovy Phonics

This /pr/ superstar is called..................................

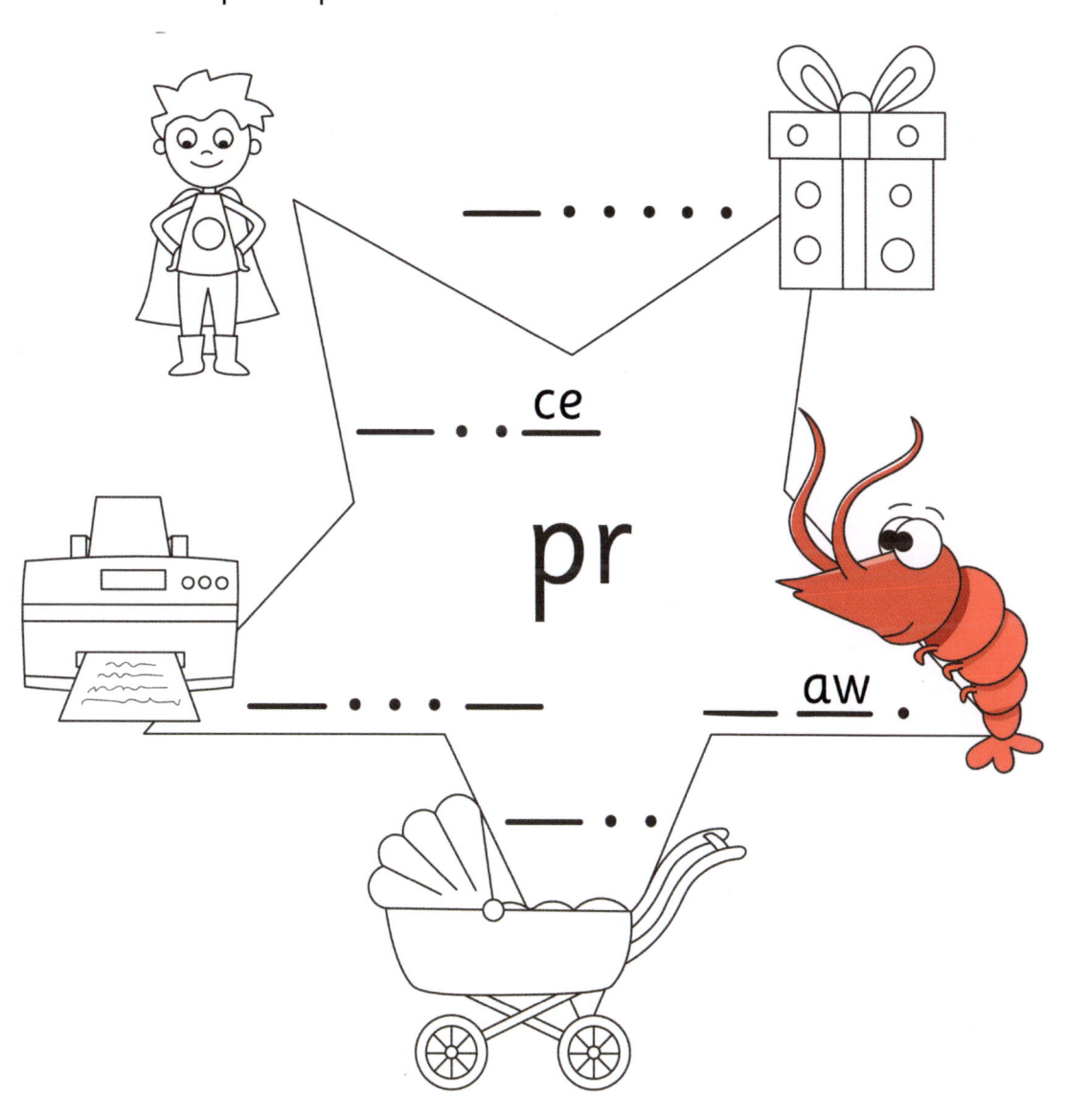

_ _ . . . . .

_ . . ce

pr

_ . . . _

_ aw .

_ . . .

Let's write a sentence using /pr/

_____

_____

Phonic flower

pr

How many words did you write?

Name: _____

Let's write a sentence using /pr/

_____

_____

Lesson plan /dr/ Dragon Drake

Hold up our Groovy Friends Dan Dinosaur and Rachel Rabbit, explain how they blend together to make our new Groovy Friend /dr/ Dragon Drake.

We find the **/dr/** sound: **mostly** at the start /dr/ip
rarely inside hun/dr/ed
never at the end

Song and dance

Teach the song and dance a line at a time as detailed on page 8.

Phonic flower prompters

If it is not wet, it is…	*dry*
We can make a hole in a wall with a…	*drill*
When it rains the water goes down the…	*drain*
Sometimes when we sleep we…	*dream*
A faulty tap might…	*drip*

Sentence modelling

Model this sentence, focus on capital letter, finger spaces and full-stop.

The dragon plays drums.

Then hand out the Phonic Challenges as Dragon Drake plays on repeat.

Plenary

Invite children to read out their sentences. Can anyone identify the /dr/ word?

tr br cr fr gr pr dr   cl fl gl pl bl sl   st sp sk sc sm sn

dr

drip

drop

drink

drum

Dragon Drake

Dragon Drake drinks juice from a plum

One hundred times he bangs on a drum

The sunroof he drops

When he drives to the shops

To buy a dreamy dress for his mum

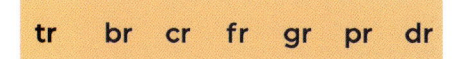

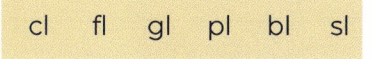

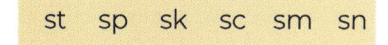

tr br cr fr gr pr dr   cl fl gl pl bl sl   st sp sk sc sm sn

1. dragon	2. drinks	3. drum	4. drops

5. drives	6. dreams	7. dress

1	Pretend to breathe fire like **Dragon Drake**.
2	Put your hand to your mouth to have a **drink**.
3	Pretend to play the **drum**.
4	Lift your raised closed hand in front of you, then open it to **drop**.
5	Pretend to **drive** your car.
6	Rest your head in your palms... sweet **dreams**.
7	Pretend to put on some clothes to **dress**.

Groovy Phonics

This /dr/ superstar is called..................................

dr

_ _ . _ .

_ . . . .

_ _ ea .

_ . . .

ea

Let's write a sentence using /dr/

_____

_____

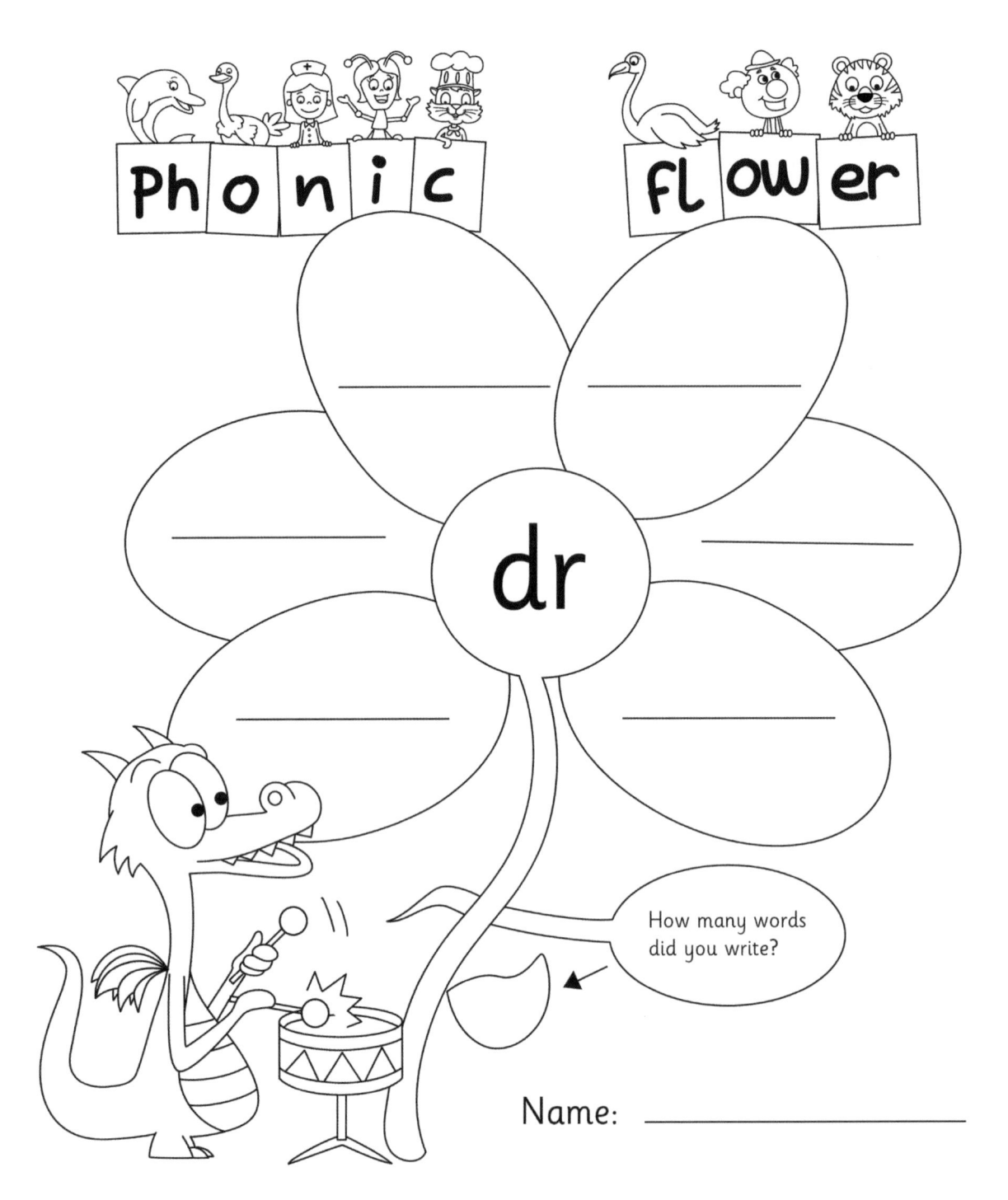

Phonic flower

dr

How many words did you write?

Name: _____

Let's write a sentence using /dr/

_____

_____

I can read 10

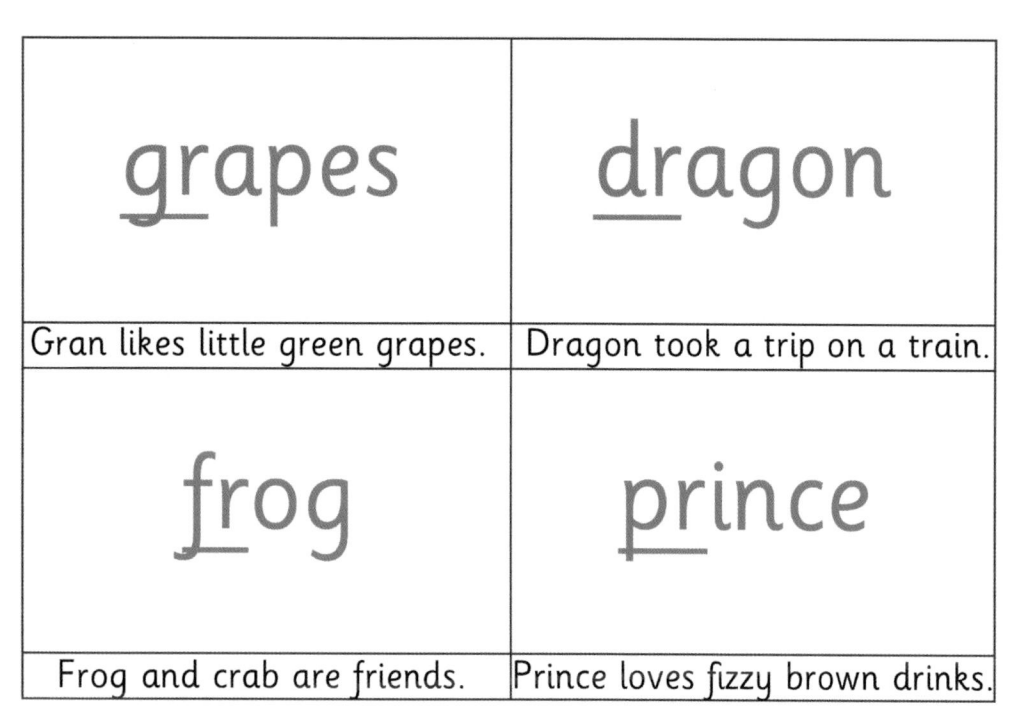

grapes	dragon
Gran likes little green grapes.	Dragon took a trip on a train.
frog	prince
Frog and crab are friends.	Prince loves fizzy brown drinks.

s e t

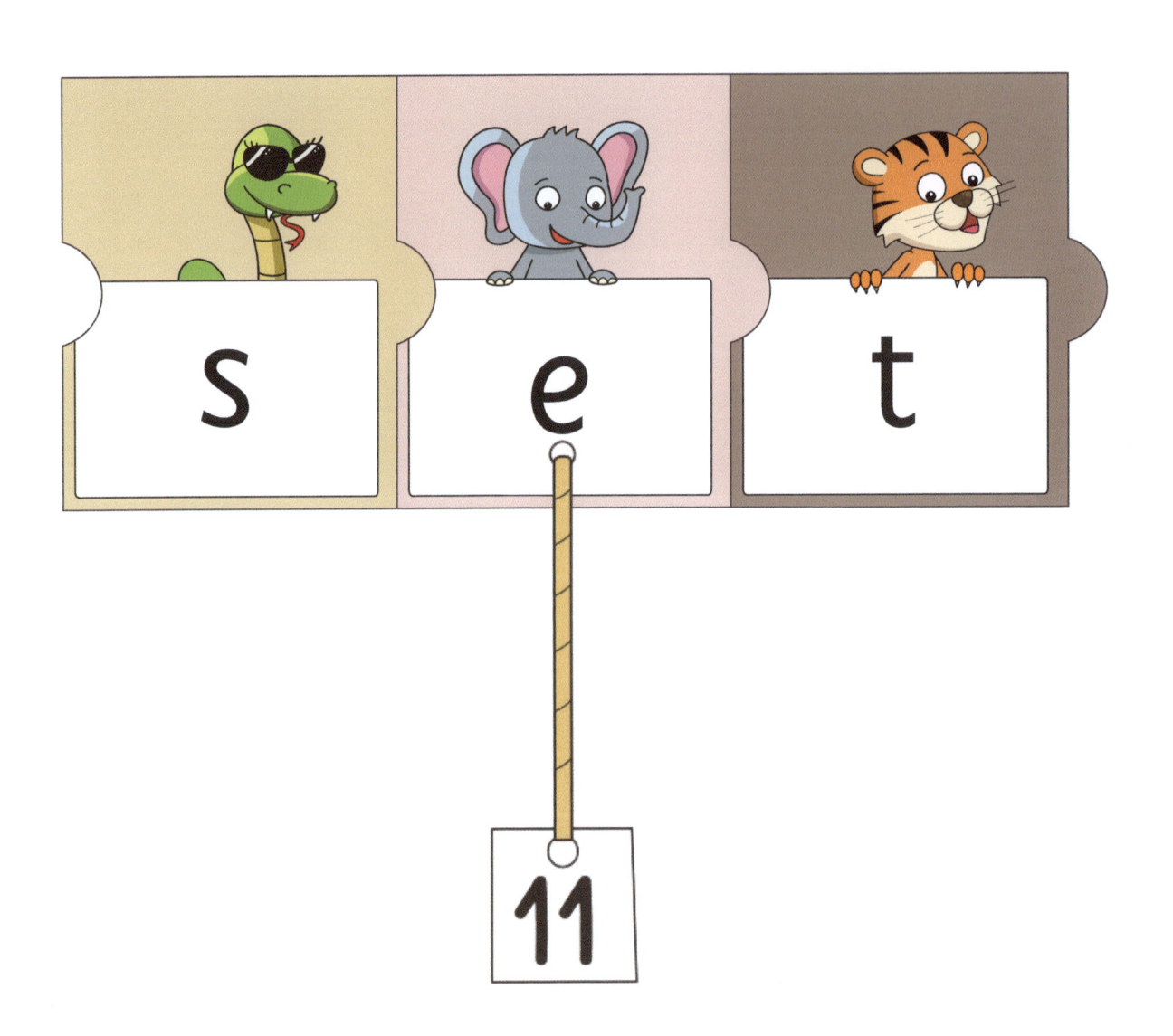

11

Lesson plan /cl/ Clara Clownfish

Hold up our Groovy Friends Casey Cat and Lenny Lizard, explain how they blend together to make the our new Groovy Friend /cl/ Clara Clownfish.

We find the **/cl/** sound: **mostly** at the start /cl/ap

rarely inside ex/cl/aim

never at the end

Song and dance

Teach the song and dance a line at a time as detailed on page 9.

Phonic flower prompters

A detective looks for…	*clues*
Dinosaurs had big…	*claws*
White fluffy things in the sky are…	*clouds*
Hickery dickery dock, the mouse ran up the…	*clock*
We are in the…	*classroom*

Sentence modelling

Model this sentence, focus on capital letter, finger spaces and full-stop.

The clever clown has funny clothes.

Hand out the Phonic Challenges as Clara Clownfish plays on repeat.

Plenary

Invite children to read out their sentences. Can anyone identify the /cl/ word?

| tr br cr fr gr pr dr | cl fl gl pl bl sl | st sp sk sc sm sn |

cl

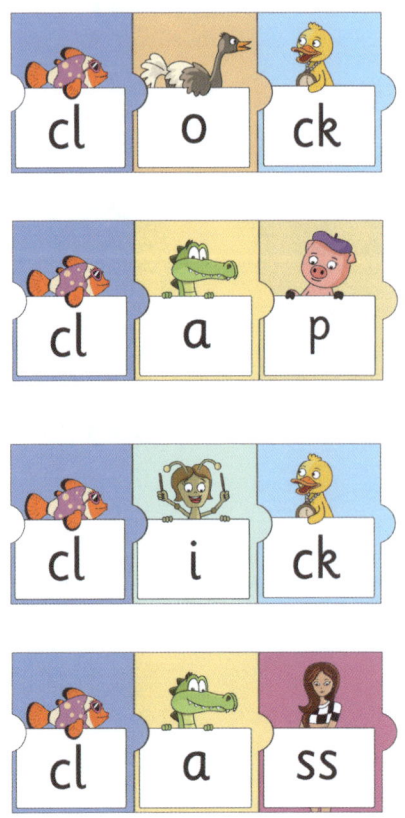

clock

clap

click

class

Clara Clownfish

Clara Clownfish loves classic clothes

The other fish clap wherever she goes

She's clearly so clever

With clean clothes forever

And closes each week with a fashion show

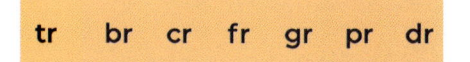

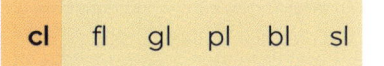

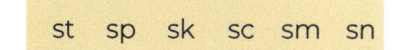

tr br cr fr gr pr dr   cl fl gl pl bl sl   st sp sk sc sm sn

| 1. clown | 2. clothes | 3. clap |
| 4. clever | 5. clean | 6. close |

1	Make a red nose fist like a **clown**.
2	Point to your **clothes**.
3	**Clap** your hands together.
4	Tap your head with your finger… so **clever**.
5	Pretend to give the table a **clean**.
6	Fold your palms together to **close** a book.

Groovy Phonics

This /cl/ superstar is called..................................

__ aw

__ ou .

cl

__ . __ .

__ ow .

__ . .

Let's write a sentence using /cl/

_____

_____

Phonic flower

cl

How many words did you write?

Name: _____

Let's write a sentence using /cl/

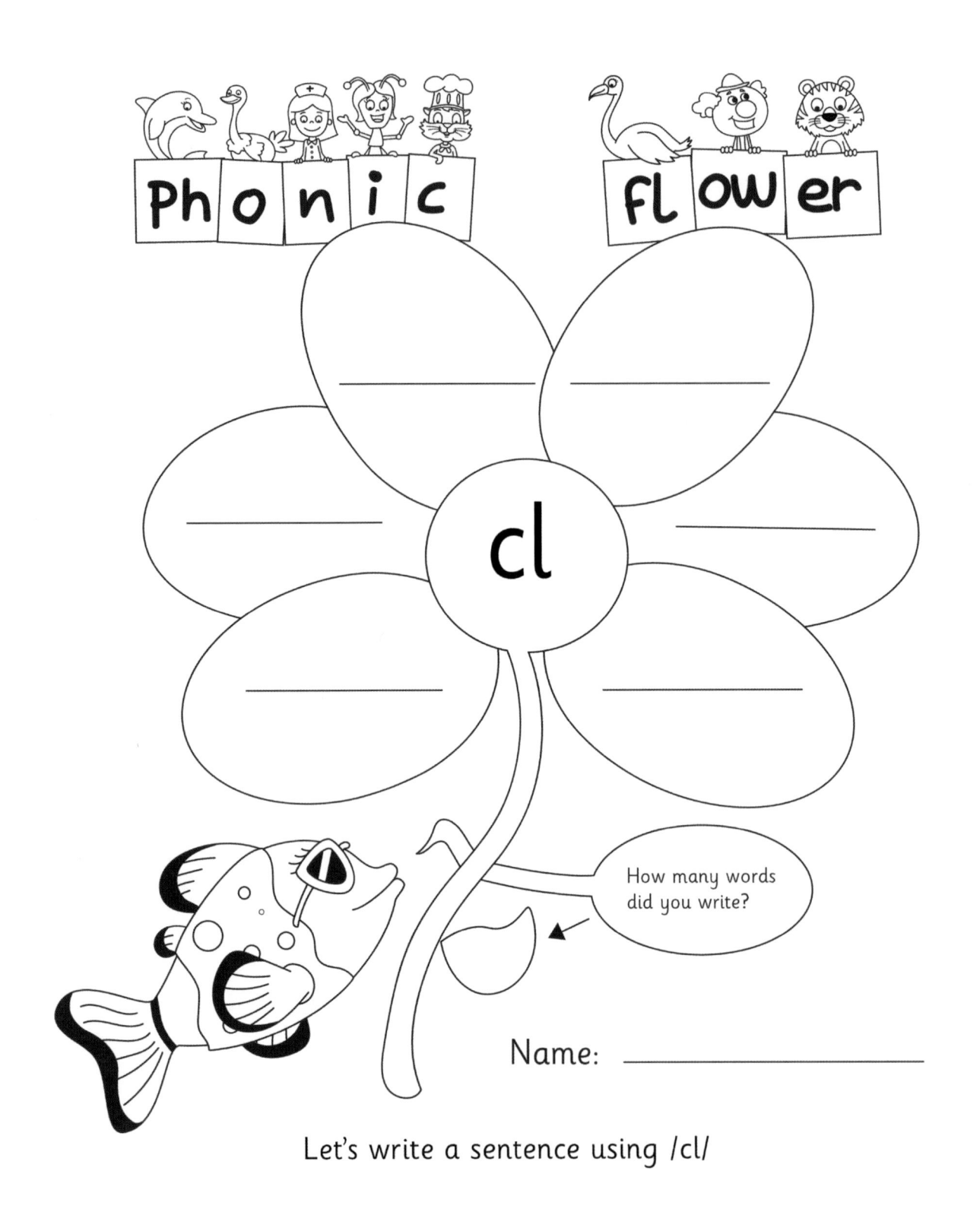

_____
_____

65

Lesson plan /fl/ Florence Flamingo

Show our Groovy Friends Freddie Frog and Lenny Lizard, explain how they blend together to make our new Groovy Friend /fl/ Florence Flamingo.

We find the **/fl/** sound: **mostly** at the start /fl/at
rarely inside in/fl/ate
never at the end

Song and dance

Teach the song and dance a line at a time as detailed on page 9.

Phonic flower prompters

At the Olympics every country waves their…	*flags*
A group of sheep is called a…	*flock*
On the beach we don't wear shoes, we wear…	*flip-flops*
We can bring water to school in a…	*flask*
Ice cream has lots of different…	*flavours*

Sentence modelling

Model this sentence, focus on capital letter, finger spaces and full-stop.

The flamingo flaps her wings.

Hand out the Phonic Challenges as Florence Flamingo plays on repeat.

Plenary

Invite children to read out their sentences. Can anyone identify the /fl/ word?

| tr br cr fr gr pr dr | cl fl gl pl bl sl | st sp sk sc sm sn |

fl

fl i p

fl a t

fl a g

fl a n

67

Florence Flamingo

Florence Flamingo walks flat on the floor

But if there's a flood, with a flash she can soar

With a flap and a flip

She's in flight super quick

Then flies back down to the flowers once more

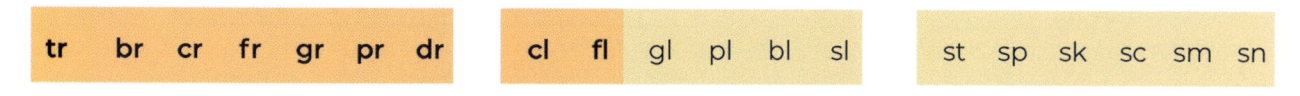

tr br cr fr gr pr dr   cl fl gl pl bl sl   st sp sk sc sm sn

68

1. flamingo   2. flat   3. floor   4. flash

5. flap   6. flight   7. flowers

1	Flap your hand wings like a **flamingo**.
2	Place your hands together **flat**.
3	Point to the **floor**.
4	Cover your eyes from the **flash**.
5	**Flap** your hand wings.
6	Put your arm wings out for **flight**.
7	Make a hand **flower**.

Groovy Phonics

This /fl/ superstar is called..

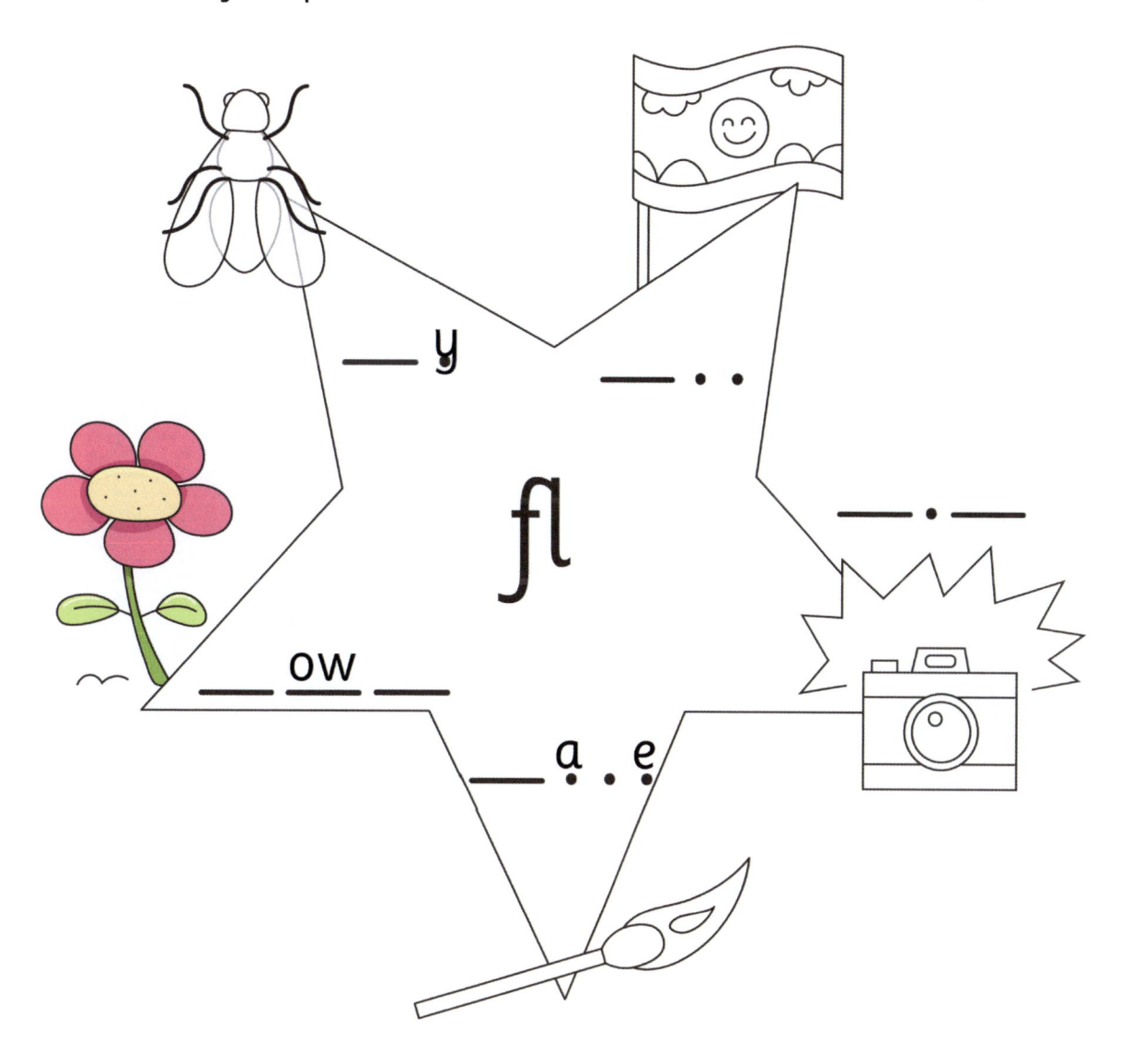

_ y

_ . .

fl

_ . _

_ ow _

_ a . e

Let's write a sentence using /fl/

_____

_____

Phonic flower

fl

How many words did you write?

Name: _____

Let's write a sentence using /fl/

_____
_____

Lesson plan /gl/ Gloria Glitterbug

Hold up our Groovy Friends Gaby Goat and Lenny Lizard, explain how they blend together to make our new Groovy Friend /gl/ Gloria Glitterbug.

We find the **/gl/** sound: **mostly** at the start /gl/ad
rarely inside u/gl/y
never at the end

Song and dance

Teach the song and dance a line at a time as detailed on page 9.

Phonic flower prompters

Windows are made of...	*glass*
If you are sad you feel...	*glum*
If you are happy you feel...	*glad*
We can stick things together with...	*glue*
A massive piece of ice is a...	*glacier*

Sentence modelling

Model this sentence, focus on capital letter, finger spaces and full-stop.

I wear gloves to wash the glasses.

Hand out the Phonic Challenges as Gloria Glitterbug plays on repeat.

Plenary

Invite children to read out their sentences. Can anyone identify the /gl/ word?

tr br cr fr gr pr dr   cl fl gl pl bl sl   st sp sk sc sm sn

72

gl

gl ow

gl a d

gl a ss

gl u m

Gloria Glitterbug

Gloria Glitterbug makes the globe glow

No gloomy nights wherever she goes

With glamourous glasses

On glorious lashes

And gloves on her hands and her toes

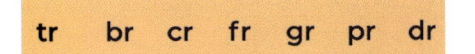

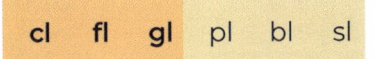

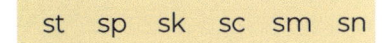

tr br cr fr gr pr dr   cl fl gl pl bl sl   st sp sk sc sm sn

| 1. glitterbug | 2. globe | 3. glow |
| 4. glasses | 5. glorious | 6. gloves |

1	Flap hand wings like **Gloria Glitterbug**.
2	Make a **globe** shape with your hands.
3	Protect your eyes from the **glow**.
4	Make an open fist for a pair of **glamorous glasses**.
5	Wave excited hands, so **glorious**.
6	Stick out your hands like you're wearing **gloves**.

Groovy Phonics

This /gl/ superstar is called..................................

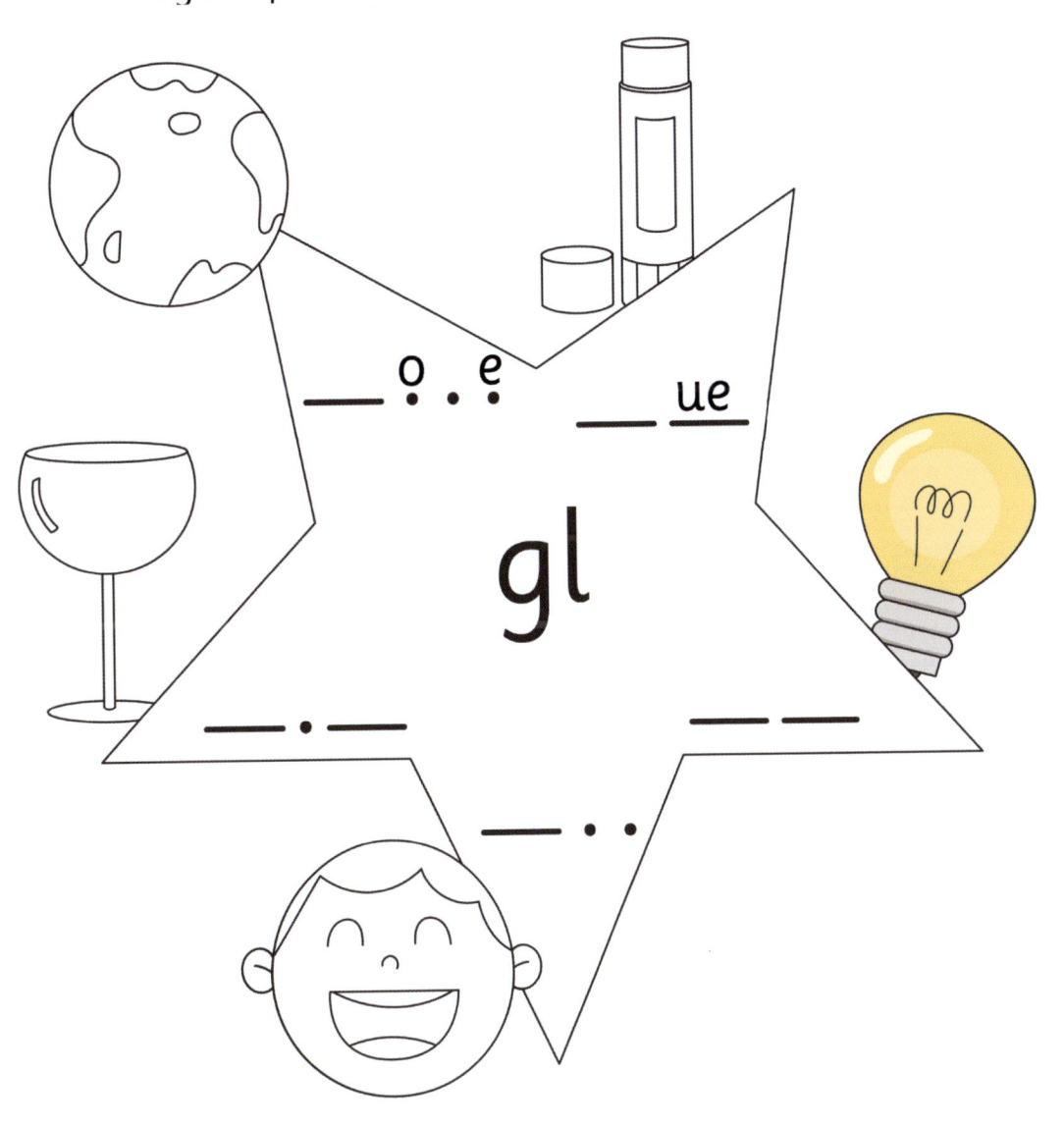

gl

Let's write a sentence using /gl/

Phonic flower

gl

How many words did you write?

Name: _____

Let's write a sentence using /gl/

_____
_____

Lesson plan /pl/ Plastic Plane

Show our Groovy Friends Penny Piglet and Lenny Lizard, explain how they blend together to make our new Groovy Friend /pl/ Plastic Plane.

We find the **/pl/** sound:
- **mostly** at the start /pl/ug
- **rarely** inside com/pl/ete
- **never** at the end

Song and dance

Teach the song and dance a line at a time as detailed on page 9.

Phonic flower prompters

In the park we love to…	*play*
We eat food on a…	*plate*
Another name for add is…	*plus*
Pirates made sailors walk the…	*plank*
Empty the sink by pulling the…	*plug*

Sentence modelling

Model this sentence, focus on capital letter, finger spaces and full-stop.

Plants on our planet are pleasant.

Hand out the Phonic Challenges as Plastic Plane plays on repeat.

Plenary

Invite children to read out their sentences. Can anyone identify the /pl/ word?

| tr br cr fr gr pr dr | cl fl gl pl bl sl | st sp sk sc sm sn |

pl

pl a n

pl u m

pl u s

pl u g

Plastic Plane

Plastic Plane came up with a plan

To fly to a place, pleasant and grand,

With plants and trees

She felt very pleased

But this planet had nowhere to land!

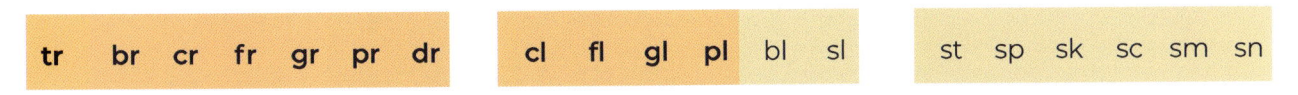

tr br cr fr gr pr dr   cl fl gl pl bl sl   st sp sk sc sm sn

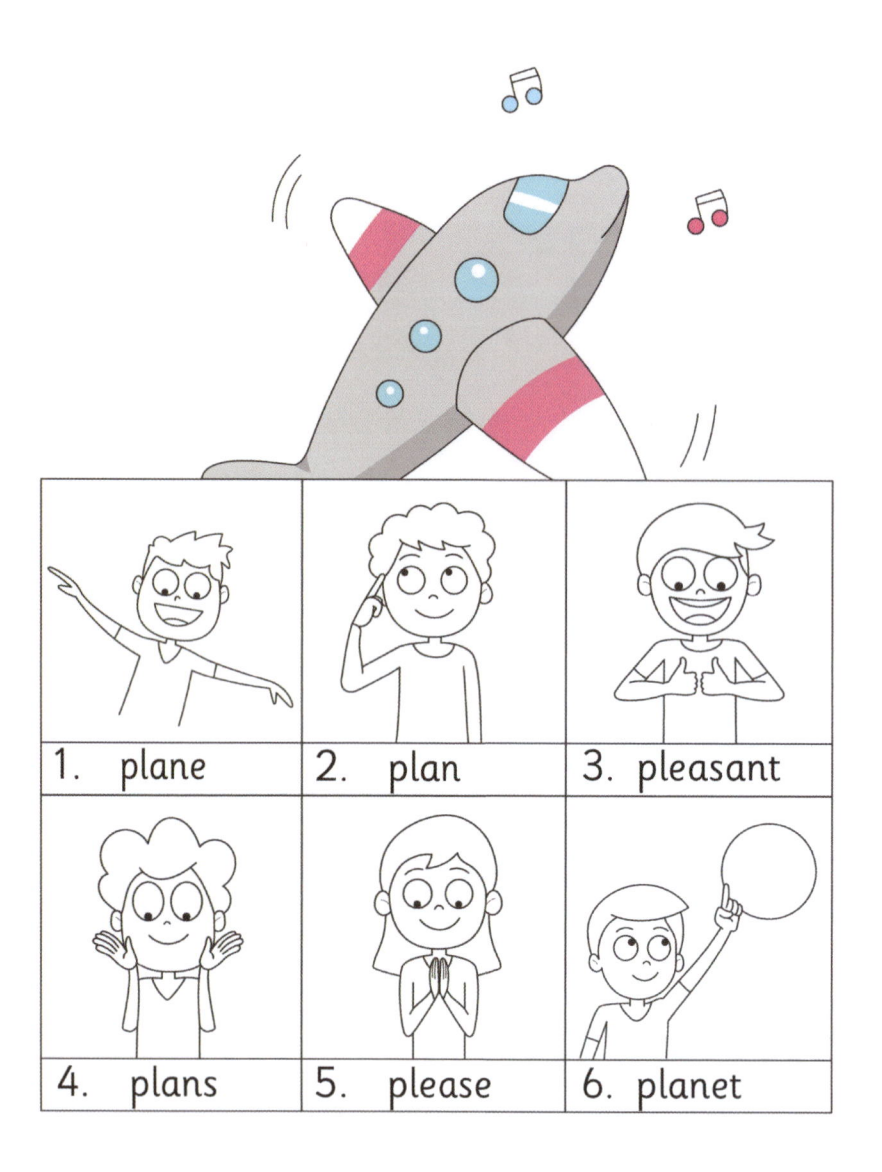

| 1. plane | 2. plan | 3. pleasant |
| 4. plans | 5. please | 6. planet |

1	Arms out like the wings of a **plane**.
2	Tap your head with your finger for a good **plan**.
3	Thumbs up for **pleasant.**
4	Make a **plant** shape with your open hands.
5	Place your palms together for **please**.
6	Make a **planet** shape with your hand.

Groovy Phonics

This /pl/ superstar is called......................................

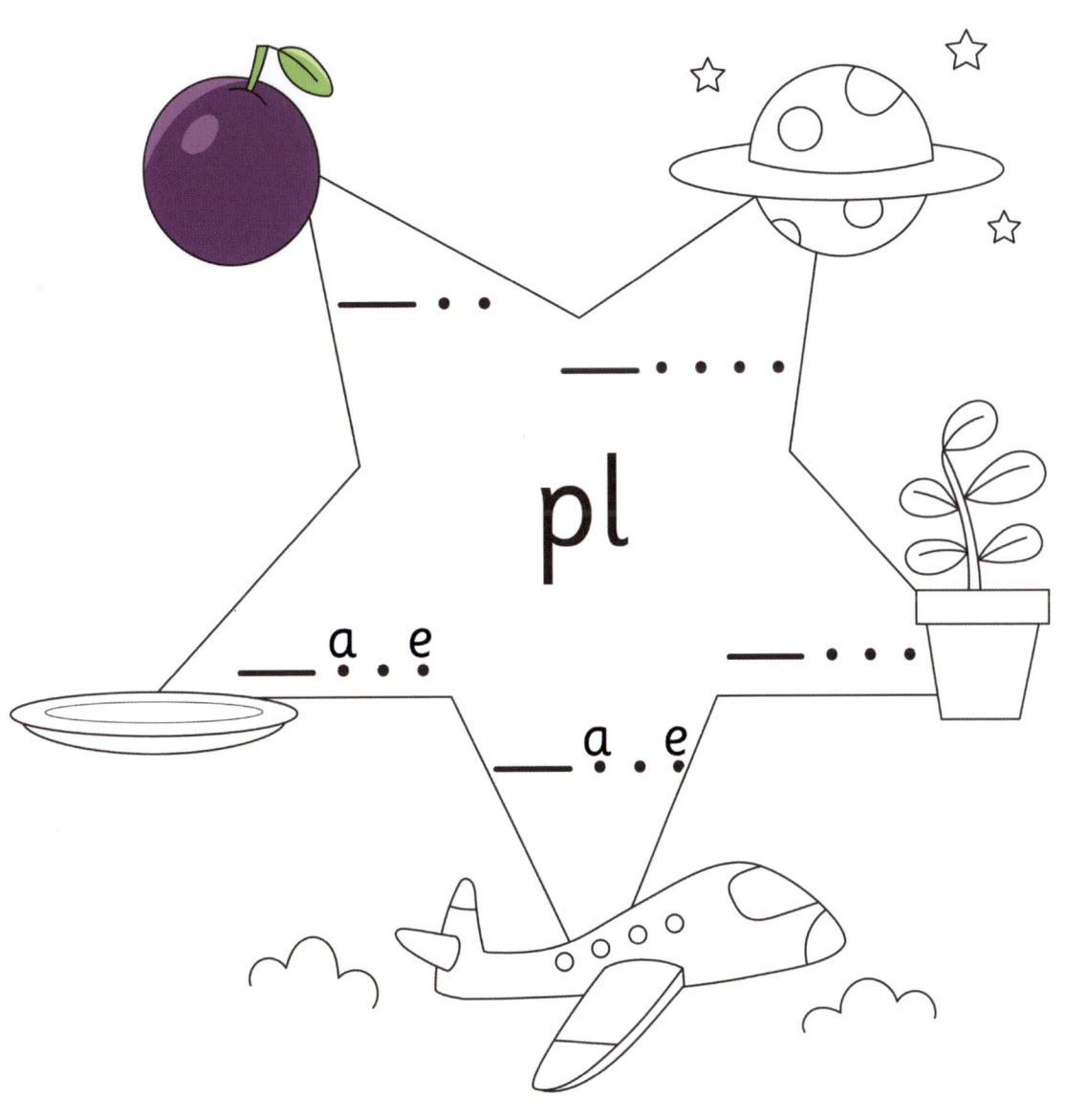

pl

_ . .
_ . . . .
_ a . e
_ . . . .
_ a . e

Let's write a sentence using /pl/

_____

_____

Phonic flower

pl

How many words did you write?

Name: _____

Let's write a sentence using /pl/

_____

_____

Lesson plan /bl/ Blake Blowfish

Show our Groovy Friends Barry Bat and Lenny Lizard, explain how they blend together to make our new Groovy Friend /bl/ Blake Blowfish.

We find the **/bl/** sound: **mostly** at the start /bl/a/ck/
  rarely inside su/bl/ime
  never at the end

Song and dance

Teach the song and dance a line at a time as detailed on page 9.

Phonic flower prompters

On our bed we have a…	*blanket*
We close both eyes quickly when we…	*blink*
We can sharpen our pencil when it's…	*blunt*
We can build models with wooden…	*blocks*
We can make smoothies in a…	*blender*

Sentence modelling

Model this sentence, focus on capital letter, finger spaces and full-stop.

My blanket is black.

Hand out the Phonic Challenges as Blake Blowfish plays on repeat.

Plenary

Invite children to read out their sentences. Can anyone identify the /bl/ word?

tr br cr fr gr pr dr   **cl fl gl pl bl** sl   st sp sk sc sm sn

bl

bl ow

bl o ck

bl a ck

bl e n d

Blake Blowfish

Blake Blowfish a **bl**end of **bl**ue and **bl**ack

His **bl**ood turns **bl**ossom when under attack

His spiky **bl**ades

Block any raid

Other fish flee like a rocket **bl**ast

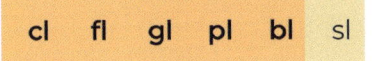

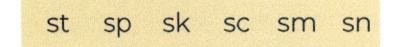

| tr br cr fr gr pr dr | cl fl gl pl bl sl | st sp sk sc sm sn |

1. blow	2. blue/black	3. blood	4. blade

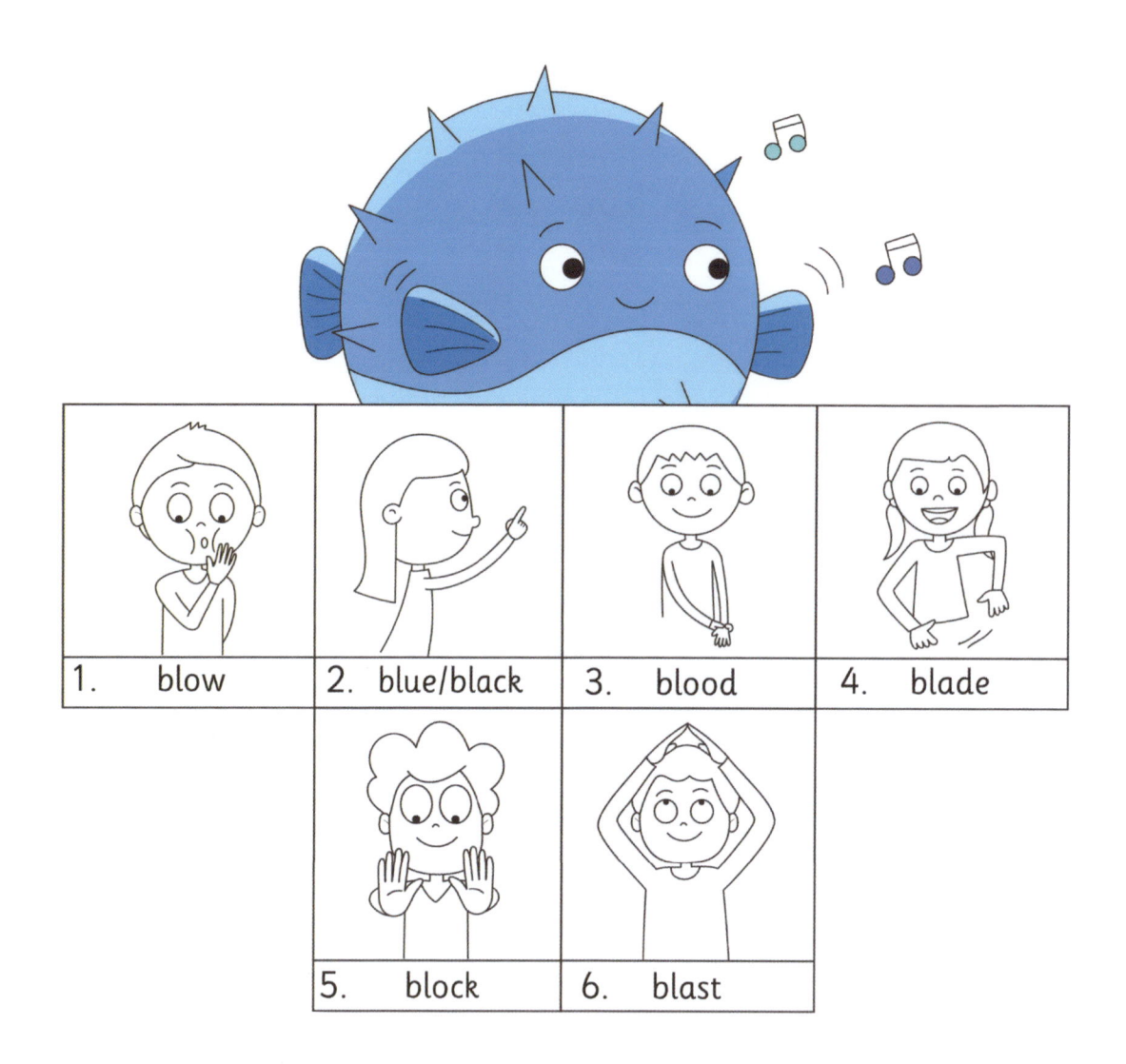

5. block	6. blast

1	**Blow** on your hands.
2	Pretend to paint with **blue** and **black**.
3	Point to your vein in your wrist, full of **blood**.
4	Pretend to swish a **blade** like a knight.
5	Raise both hands to **block**.
6	**Blast** off like a rocket.

Groovy Phonics

This /bl/ superstar is called……………………………

_ue

bl

Let's write a sentence using /bl/

_____

_____

Phonic flower

bl

How many words did you write?

Name: _____

Let's write a sentence using /bl/

_____

_____

89

Lesson plan /sl/ Sleepy Sloth

Show our Groovy Friends Sophie Snake and Lenny Lizard, explain how they blend together to make our new Groovy Friend /sl/ Sleepy Sloth.

We find the **/sl/** sound: **mostly** at the start /sl/ip
 rarely inside a/sl/eep
 never at the end

Song and dance

Teach the song and dance a line at a time as detailed on page 9.

Phonic flower prompters

Snakes don't walk they...	*slither*
If you break you arm, you rest it in a...	*sling*
A fox is very...	*sly*
A shirt has two...	*sleeves*
You drop money in a piggy bank through the...	*slot*

Sentence modelling

Model this sentence, focus on capital letter, finger spaces and full-stop.

A sloth is slow.

Hand out the Phonic Challenges as Sleepy Sloth plays on repeat.

Plenary

Invite children to read out their sentences. Can anyone identify the /sl/ word?

tr br cr fr gr pr dr	cl fl gl pl bl sl	st sp sk sc sm sn

sl

sl ow

sl a p

sl i p

sl ee p

Sleepy Sloth

Sleepy Sloth, Sleepy Sloth, wears slippers all day

Then slides down a slope on a slippery sleigh

Slow slug who is nice

Then cuts him a slice

Of slime cake, that slips right off the tray

| tr br cr fr gr pr dr | cl fl gl pl bl sl | st sp sk sc sm sn |

1. sleepy	2. slippers	3. slides
4. slug	5. slice	6. slime

1	Rest your head against your palms, so **sleepy**.
2	Point to the **slippers** on your feet.
3	Arms swinging like sliding down a **slope**.
4	Make finger antennae like a **slug**.
5	Make a triangular **slice** of cake.
6	Pretend to be stretching some **slime**.

Groovy Phonics

This /sl/ superstar is called ....

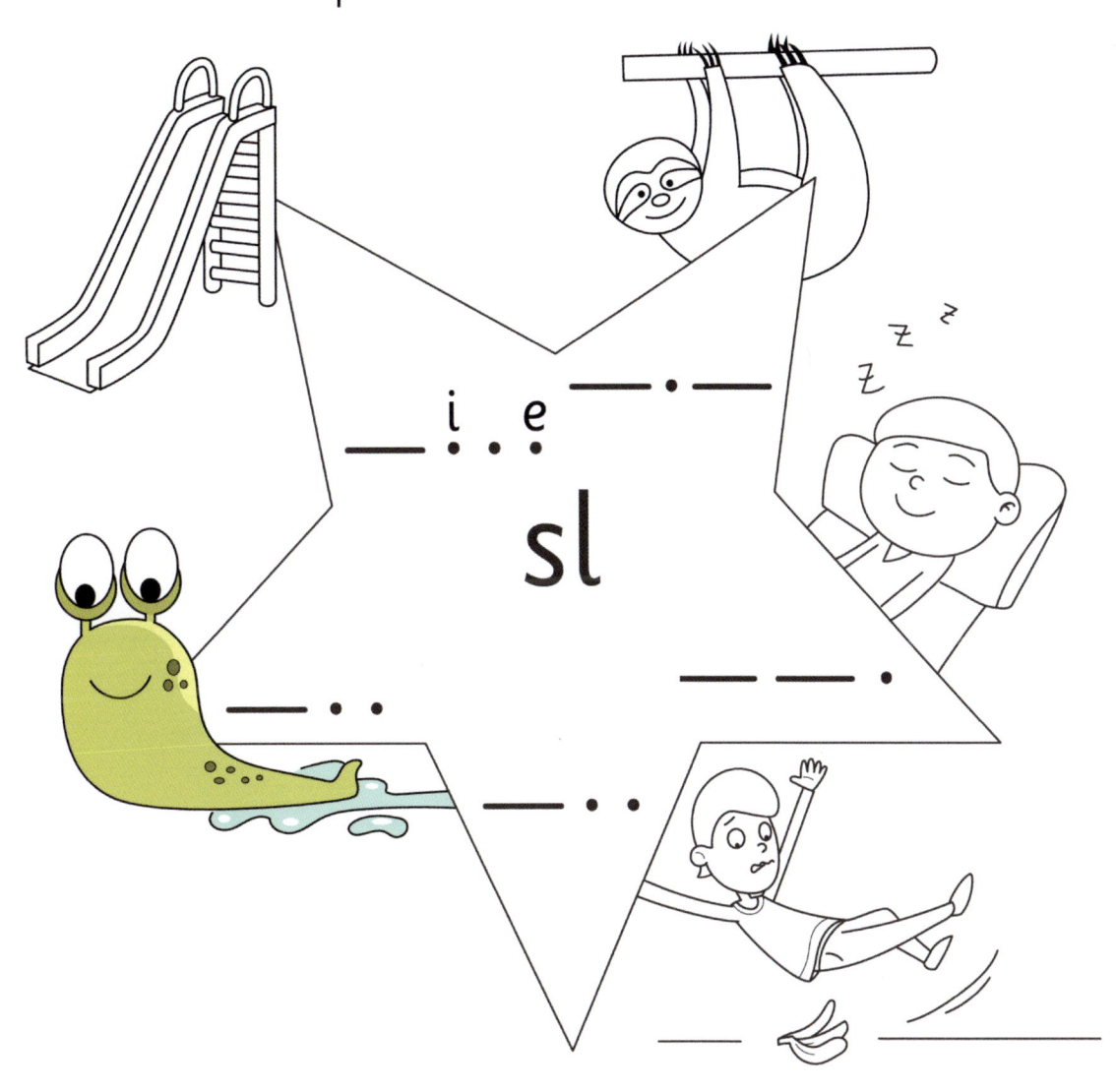

sl

Let's write a sentence using /sl/

_____

_____

Phonic flower

sl

How many words did you write?

Name: _____

Let's write a sentence using /sl/

_____
_____

I can read 11

flag	**plane**
One flag with a flower.	The plane is clean and blue.
slipper	**clouds**
Slug sleeps in a glass slipper.	Clouds blow so slowly.

s e t

12

Lesson plan /st/ Steve Stegosaurus

Show our Groovy Friends Sophie Snake and Tommy Tiger, explain how they blend together to make our new Groovy Friend /st/ Steve Stegosaurus.

We find the **/st/** sound: **mostly** at the start /st/ep
sometimes inside mon/st/er
sometimes at the end fa/st/

Song and dance

Teach the song and dance a line at a time as detailed on page 9.

Phonic flower prompters

In the park dogs love to fetch…	*sticks*
A fun party game is called musical….	*statues*
We stand still like a statue when the music…	*stops*
If we behave well at school we might get a…	*sticker*
A cheetah can run really….	*fast*

Sentence modelling

Model this sentence, focus on capital letter, finger spaces and full-stop.

I put stickers on my star.

Hand out the Phonic Challenges as Steve Stegosaurus plays on repeat.

Plenary

Invite children to read out their sentences. Can anyone identify the /st/ word?

| tr | br | cr | fr | gr | pr | dr |

| cl | fl | gl | pl | bl | sl |

| **st** | sp | sk | sc | sm | sn |

st

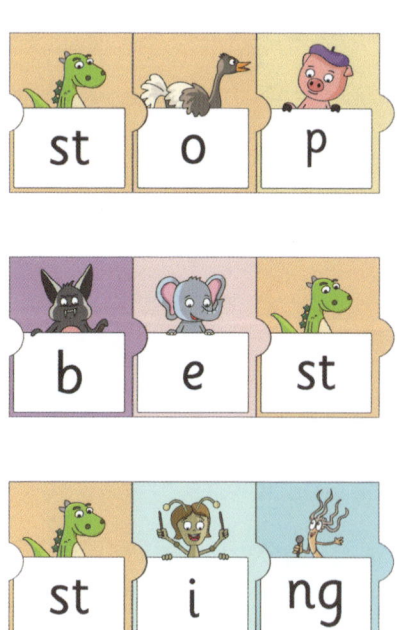

st o p

b e st

st i ng

st i ck

99

Steve Stegosaurus

Steve Stegosaurus loves breakfast the most

He just never stops feasting on toast

He stands taller than cars

With monster plate stars

"Forget the rest, I'm the best!" he boasts

tr br cr fr gr pr dr   cl fl gl pl bl sl   st sp sk sc sm sn

1. stegosaurus	2. breakfast	3. most	4. stops
5. toast	6. monster	7. stars	8. rest	9. best

1	Make hand spikes on your head like **Steve Stegosaurus.**
2	Rub your tummy, mmm... **breakfast.**
3	Thumbs up for loving the **most.**
4	Show your raised palm for **stop.**
5	Straight hands like **toast** popping out of the **toaster.**
6	Make scary hand claws like a **monster.**
7	Open and close your hands like sparkling **stars.**
8	Point backwards with your thumbs for the **rest.**
9	Make the a-ok sign with your thumb and forefinger for **best.**

Groovy Phonics

This /st/ superstar is called..................................

st

Let's write a sentence using /st/

_____
_____

Phonic flower

st

How many words did you write?

Name: _____

Let's write a sentence using /st/

Lesson plan /sp/ Spencer Spider

Show our Groovy Friends Sophie Snake and Penny Piglet, explain how they blend together to make our new Groovy Friend /sp/ Spencer Spider.

We find the **/sp/** sound:
- **mostly** at the start /sp/ot
- **rarely** inside whi/sp/er
- **rarely** at the end wa/sp/

Song and dance

Teach the song and dance a line at a time as detailed on page 9.

Phonic flower prompters

We wash the dishes with a...	*sponge*
The season when flowers bloom is...	*spring*
A poisonous snake might...	*spit*
We dig at the beach with a bucket and...	*spade*
A sunny country that is popular for holidays is...	*Spain*

Sentence modelling

Model this sentence, focus on capital letter, finger spaces and full-stop.

The spider spins a web.

Hand out the Phonic Challenges as the Spencer Spider song plays on repeat.

Plenary

Invite children to read out their sentences. Can anyone identify the /sp/ word?

| tr | br | cr | fr | gr | pr | dr | | cl | fl | gl | pl | bl | sl | | st | sp | sk | sc | sm | sn |

sp

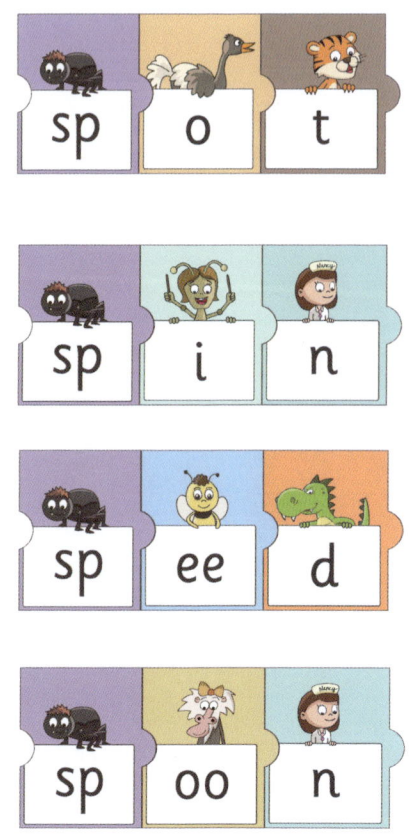

sp o t

sp i n

sp ee d

sp oo n

Spencer Spider

Spencer Spider has a special spotty spear

To spike flies and wasps whenever they're near

He eats with a spoon

Spins a web on the moon

To spend a spell in space every year

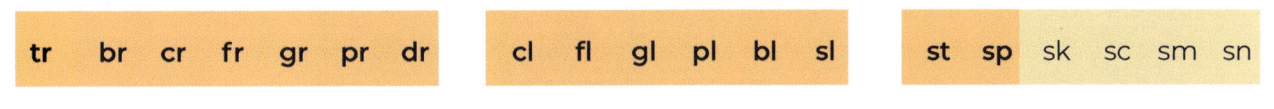

tr br cr fr gr pr dr   cl fl gl pl bl sl   st sp sk sc sm sn

1	Pretend your hand is a **spider**.
2	Make **spots** on your arm by dabbing it with your finger tips.
3	Pretend to be throwing a **spear**.
4	Make **spikes** on your head with an open hand.
5	Buzz your hand wings like a **wasp**.
6	Place a **spoon** to your mouth.
7	Make a planet shape in the air for **space**.

Groovy Phonics

This /sp/ superstar is called..................................

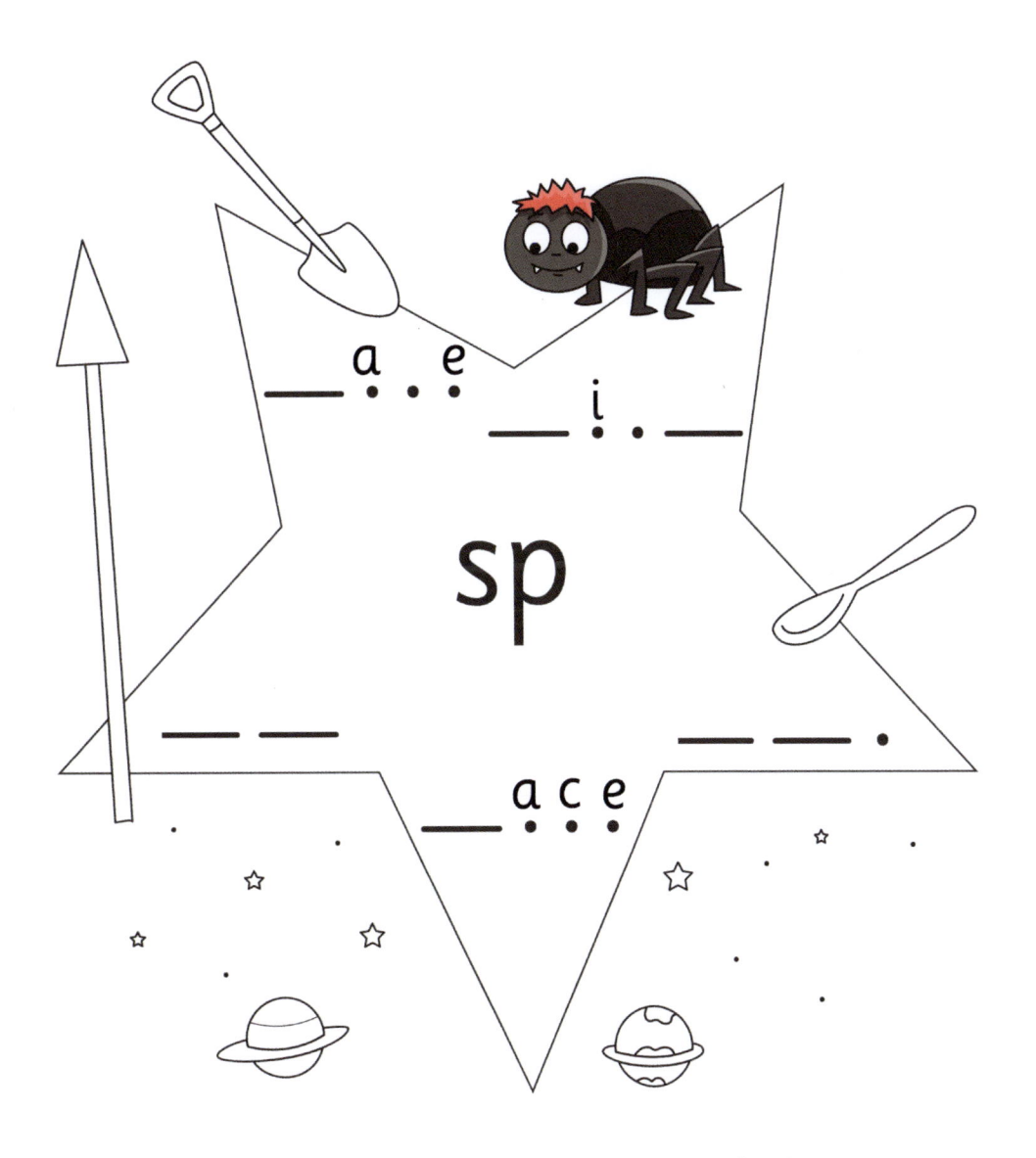

sp

_ a _ e
. . .

_ i _

_ _

_ _ .

_ a c e _
. . .

Let's write a sentence using /sp/

_____

_____

108

Phonic Flower

sp

How many words did you write?

Name: _____

Let's write a sentence using /sp/

_____
_____

Lesson plan /sk/ Skeleton Skipp

Show our Groovy Friends Sophie Snake and Ken Kangaroo, explain how they blend together to make our new Groovy Friend /sk/ Skeleton Skipp.

We find the **/sk/** sound: **mostly** at the start /sk/in

rarely at the end a/sk/

rarely in the middle water/sk/i

Song and dance

Teach the song and dance a line at a time as detailed on page 9.

Phonic flower prompters

Our bodies are covered in…	*skin*
A smelly black and white animal is a…	*skunk*
When drawing, we use a pencil to…	*sketch*
A fun bowling game is called…	*skittles*
The captain on a boat is the…	*skipper*

Sentence modelling

Model this sentence, focus on capital letter, finger spaces and full-stop.

I like to skip.

Hand out the Phonic Challenges as Skeleton Skipp plays on repeat.

Plenary

Invite children to read out their sentences. Can anyone identify the /sk/ word?

tr br cr fr gr pr dr   cl fl gl pl bl sl   st sp sk sc sm sn

sk

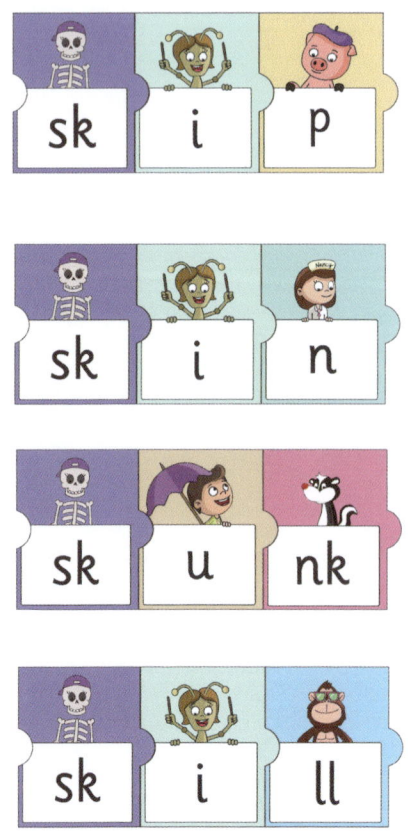

sk i p

sk i n

sk u nk

sk i ll

111

Skeleton Skipp

Skeleton Skipp loves to roller skate

Skidding about with her skinny mates

They love to ski too

In skimpy skirts blue

With hats on their skulls as they race

tr br cr fr gr pr dr   cl fl gl pl bl sl   st sp sk sc sm sn

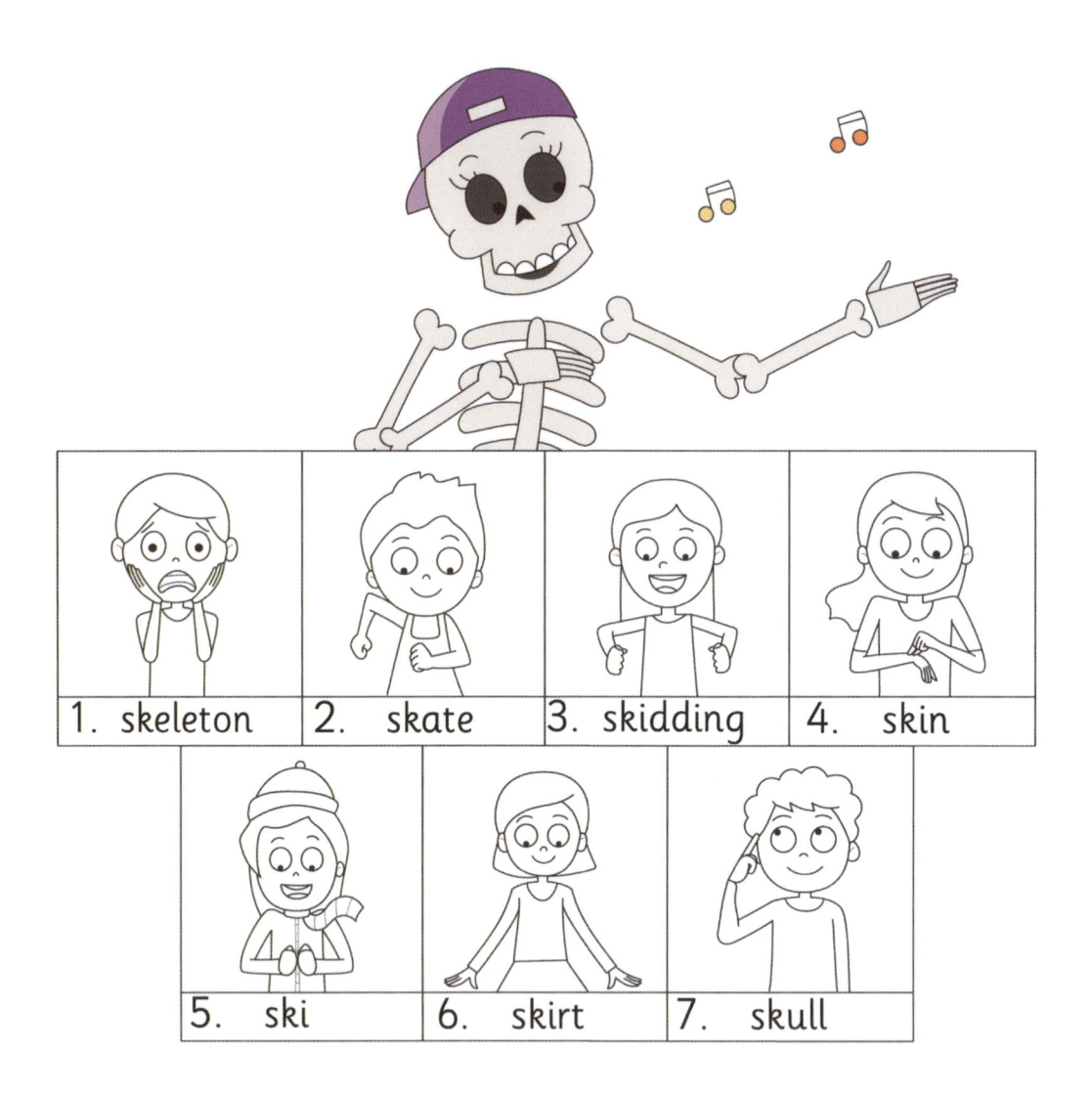

1. skeleton
2. skate
3. skidding
4. skin
5. ski
6. skirt
7. skull

1	Squeeze you face with your hands like a **Skeleton Skipp**.
2	Move your arms back and forth to **skate**.
3	Pretend to be steering a **skidding** car.
4	Move both your arms simultaneously to **ski**.
5	Fan your hands by your sides like a **skirt**.
6	With your fingertip, tap your **skull**.

Groovy Phonics

This /sk/ superstar is called……………………………………

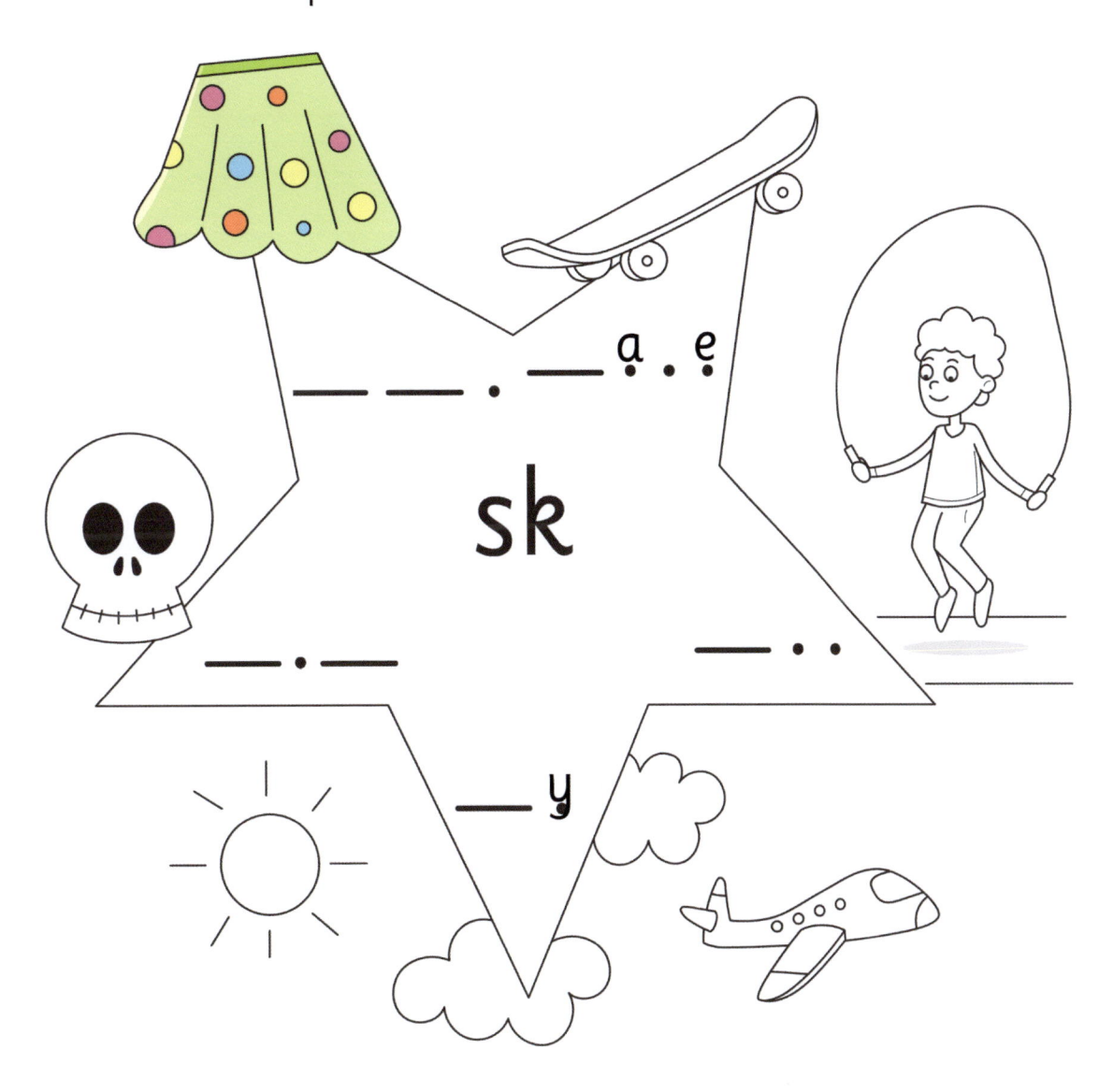

sk

_ _ _ _ . _ a_ . e_

_ . _ _ . .

_ y

Let's write a sentence using /sk/

_____

_____

Phonic flower

sk

How many words did you write?

Name: _____

Let's write a sentence using /sk/

115

Lesson plan /sc/ Scarlett Scout

Show our Groovy Friend Skeleton Skipp and review the sound /sk/. Now model how there is another way to make this same sound by combining Sophie Snake and Casey Cat to make our new Groovy Friend /sc/ Scarlett Scout.

We find the **/sc/** sound: **mostly** at the start /sc/arf

rarely inside e/sc/ape

never at the end...

Song and dance

Teach the song and dance a line at a time as detailed on page 9.

Phonic flower prompters

A farmer frightens away birds with a...	*scarecrow*
We put on a snorkel and mask in the sea to...	*scuba*
It is fun to ride on a two wheel...	*scooter*
When we play sport we try to...	*score*
A little desert creature with a stinging tail is a...	*scorpion*

Sentence modelling

Model this sentence, focus on capital letter, finger spaces and full-stop.

A scarecrow on a scooter!

Hand out the Phonic Challenges as Scarlett Scout plays on repeat.

Plenary

Invite children to read out their sentences. Can anyone identify the /sc/ word? Now can they remember a /sk/ word too?

| tr | br | cr | fr | gr | pr | dr |

| cl | fl | gl | pl | bl | sl |

| st | sp | sk | sc | sm | sn |

sc

sc ar

sc ar f

sc a n

sc oo p

Scarlett Scout

Scarlett Scout with her scarf and coat

Scans Scotland with her telescope

A scaly long neck

Made her scream so red

"Loch Ness is so scary!" she croaked

1. scout 2. scarf 3. telescope 4. scales

5. scream 6. scary

1	Make a three finger salute like a **scout**.
2	Wrap a **scarf** around your neck.
3	Use your open fists to make a **telescope**.
4	Link your fingers, elbows out, to make a **scale**.
5	Hold your face in your hands to **scream**.
6	Make a **scary** face.

Groovy Phonics

This /sc/ superstar is called..................................

_ _ _ ou .

_ _ _ .

sc

_ _ a.e. _

..... _ o.e.

Let's write a sentence using /sc/

_____

_____

Phonic flower

SC

How many words did you write?

Name: _____

Let's write a sentence using /sc/

Lesson plan /sm/ Smith Smew

Show our Groovy Friends Sophie Snake and Matty Monkey, explain how they blend together to make our new Groovy Friend /sm/ Smith Smew. Explain that a smew is a black and white duck.

We find the **/sm/** sound:	**only** at the start /sm/art
	never inside
	never at the end

Song and dance

Teach the song and dance a line at a time as detailed on page 9.

Phonic flower prompters

Fire causes lots of…	*smoke*
On school photo day we should look…	*smart*
When we paint we should wear a…	*smock*
Dirty pollution is called…	*smog*
If you rub your pencil work it will…	*smudge*

Sentence modelling

Model this sentence, focus on capital letter, finger spaces and full-stop.

This smoothie smells great.

Hand out the Phonic Challenges as Smith Smew plays on repeat.

Plenary

Invite children to read out their sentences. Can anyone identify the /sm/ word?

| tr br cr fr gr pr dr | cl fl gl pl bl sl | st sp sk sc sm sn |

sm

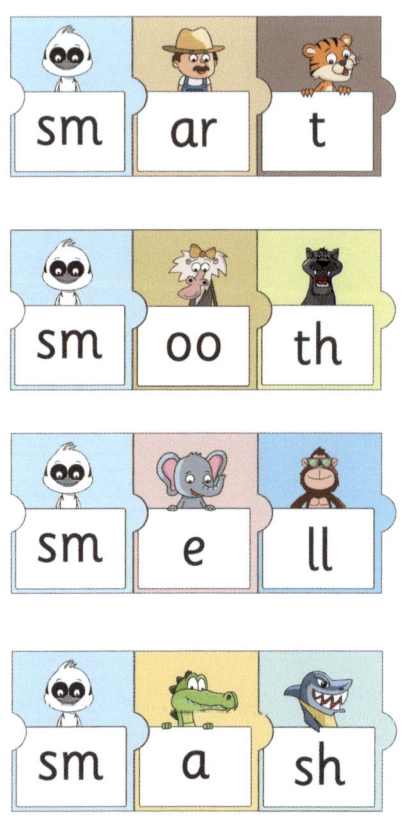

- sm ar t
- sm oo th
- sm e ll
- sm a sh

Smith Smew

Smith the smew a duck oh so smart

Smooth zebra feathers in every part

He smiles oh so cute

While smashing up fruit

For smoothies and small smelly tarts

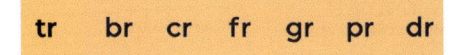

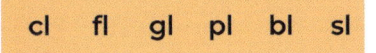

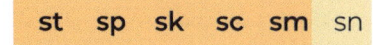

tr br cr fr gr pr dr   cl fl gl pl bl sl   st sp sk sc sm sn

1. smew	2. smart	3. smooth	4. smile
5. smash	6. small	7. smelly	

1	Make a hand duck beak like **Smith Smew**.
2	Tug your lapels, so **smart**.
3	Stroke your forearm, so **smooth**.
4	Point to your big **smile**.
5	**Smash** your fist into your palm.
6	Make a **small** space with your finger and thumb.
7	Waft your hand in front of your face, so **smelly**.

Groovy Phonics

This /sm/ superstar is called..............................

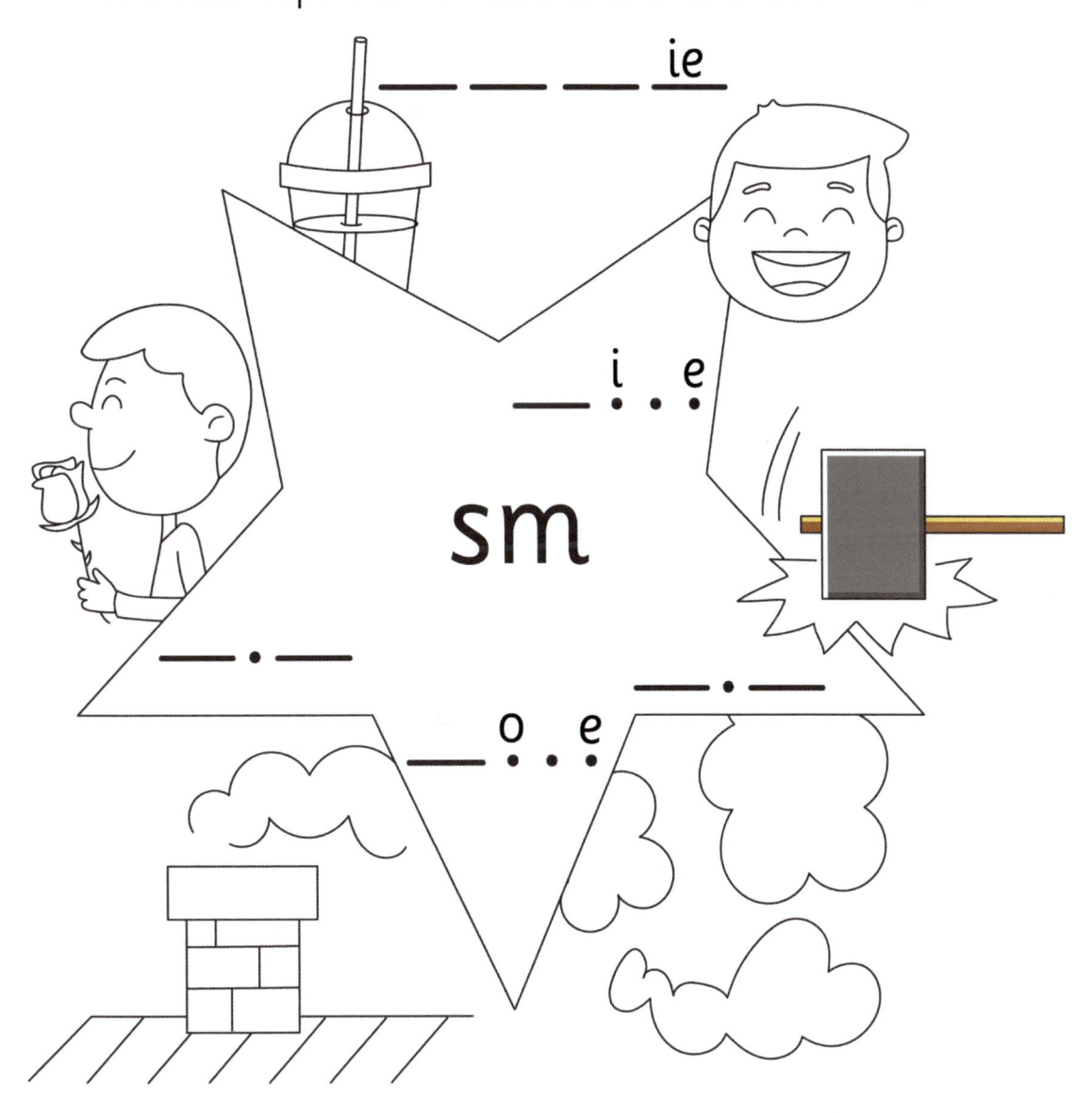

_ _ _ _ ie

_ _ i _ e

sm

_ _ . _

_ _ o _ e

Let's write a sentence using /sm/

_____

_____

126

Phonic flower

sm

How many words did you write?

Name: _____

Let's write a sentence using /sm/

_____
_____

Lesson plan /sn/ Sniffy Snowman

Show our Groovy Friends Sophie Snake and Nancy Nurse, explain how they blend together to make our new Groovy Friend /sn/ Sniffy Snowman.

We find the **/sn/** sound: **only** at the start /sn/ap
                                never inside
                                never at the end

Song and dance

Teach the song and dance a line at a time as detailed on page 9.

Phonic flower prompters

A little cut with scissors is a...	*snip*
A pig's nose is called a...	*snout*
We can call sports shoes, trainers or...	*sneakers*
Charlie Brown's dog is called...	*Snoopy*
When some people sleep they...	*snore*

Sentence modelling

Model this sentence, focus on capital letter, finger spaces and full-stop.

Snow makes me sneeze.

Hand out the Phonic Challenges as Sniffy Snowman plays on repeat.

Plenary

Invite children to read out their sentences. Can anyone identify the /sn/ word?

tr br cr fr gr pr dr   cl fl gl pl bl sl   st sp sk sc sm sn

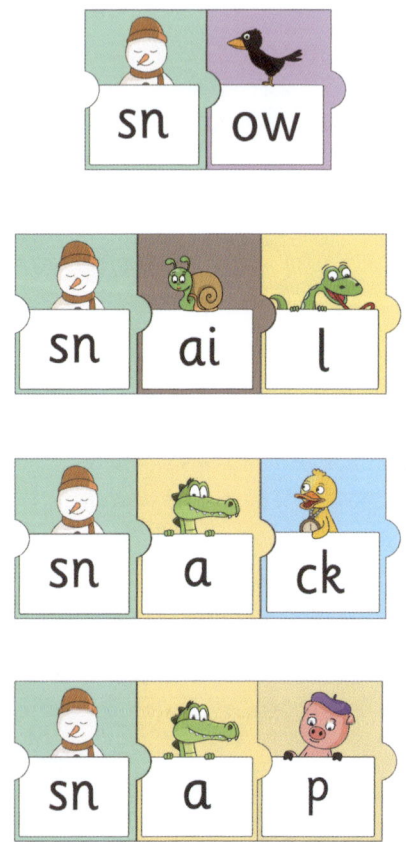

sn

sn ow

sn ai l

sn a ck

sn a p

Sniffy Snowman

Sniffy Snowman had a strange snoozy dream

About a snack eating snake munching ice cream

And a snood wearing snail

Snorkelling with a whale

Then she woke with a snap and a sneeze

tr br cr fr gr pr dr   cl fl gl pl bl sl   st sp sk sc sm sn

1. snow	2. snooze	3. snack	4. snake
5. snail	6. snorkle	7. snap	8. sneeze

1	Hug yourself warm for **snow**.
2	Rest your head on your palms for **snooze**.
3	Hands to your mouth for a **snack**.
4	Slither your hands like a **snake**.
5	Make finger antennae like a **snail**.
6	Pinch your nose and raise your hand like a **snorkel**.
7	Pretend to **snap** something in half.
8	Put your hands to your nose and pretend to **sneeze**.

Groovy Phonics

This /sn/ superstar is called..................................

sn

a e

Let's write a sentence using /sn/

_____

_____

Phonic flower

sn

How many words did you write?

Name: _____

Let's write a sentence using /sn/

_____

_____

133

I can read 12

spider	skin
Spider spun a smart web.	Snake has scaly spotty skin.
snail	scarf
Snail stopped for a snack.	Snow sticks to my scarf.

Groovy Phonics: Assessment 3

Set 10

| tr | br | cr | fr | gr | pr | dr |

| train | bring | cross | fright | green | print | drag |

The prince drew one hundred bright green trees.

Set 11

| cl | fl | gl | pl | bl | sl |

| clear | flight | glow | plant | black | sleep |

The firefly glows slowly in the clear blue sky.

Set 12

| st | sk | sc | sp | sm | sn |

| stop | skin | scab | spin | smell | snow |

The wasp skids and spins in the snowstorm.

Secret words

said	so	have	like	some	come
love	do	were	here	little	says
there	when	what	one	out	today

Name:

Groovy Friends

tr

br

cr

fr

gr

pr

dr

cr	br	tr
pr	gr	fr
		dr

cl

fl

gl

pl

bl

gl fl cl

bl pl

sl

st

sp

sk

sc

sm

sn

sp st sl

sm sc sk

sn

Secret Words

Cut out and laminate and practise every day:

said	so	have
like	some	come
love	do	were

here	little	says
there	when	what
one	out	today

Groovy Phonics

Book 1 — Teaching phonics through song and dance

Book 2 — Teaching phonics through song and dance

Book 3 — Teaching phonics through song and dance

Book 4 — Teaching phonics through song and dance

Printed in Great Britain
by Amazon